BACKYARD SAFARIS:

52 Year-Round Science Adventures

BACKYARD SAFARIS:

52 Year-Round Science Adventures

by Phyllis S. Busch

illustrated by Wayne J. Trimm

SIMON & SCHUSTER BOOKS FOR YOUNG READERS

The author owes the completion of this book to the faith and encouragement of her dear friend Richard Grossman.

SIMON & SCHUSTER BOOKS FOR YOUNG READERS
An imprint of Simon & Schuster Children's Publishing Division
1230 Avenue of the Americas, New York, New York 10020

SIMON & SCHUSTER BOOKS FOR YOUNG READERS
is a trademark of Simon & Schuster.

Book design by Jo Anne Metsch
The text for this book is set in ITC Garamond.
The illustrations are rendered in pencil and watercolor.
Manufactured in the United States of America
First edition
10 9 8 7 6 5 4 3 2 1

Library of Congress Cataloging-in-Publication Data
Busch, Phyllis S.
Backyard safaris: 52 year-round science adventures /
by Phyllis S. Busch. – 1st ed.
p. cm.
Includes index.
ISBN 0-689-80302-8
1. Natural history–Juvenile literature. 2. Seasons–Juvenile literature.
3. Natural history–Study and teaching–Activity programs–Juvenile literature.
[1. Nature study. 2. Seasons.]
I. Title
QH48.B9755 1995   93-48410
508–dc20

For Lancelee James Trimm
        —P. S. B.

To everyone who finds joy and
inspiration in nature
        —W. J. T.

The most precious things of life are near at hand, without money and without price. Each of you has the whole wealth of the universe at your very door. All that I ever had, may be yours by stretching forth your hand and taking it.

–JOHN BURROUGHS

AN INVITATION TO GO ON SAFARI

Come. I wish to take a walk with you.
        Please come.
We'll look at the old and find what's new.

Come. No need for faraway places.
        Do come.
Our backyards have many wild spaces.

Come. Let's go outside to see what's there.
        So come.
Search for violets; hunt the woolly bear.

Come. Explore a pond and life in a tree.
        Please come.
Much more's in store when on safari.

                                    —P. S. B.

Contents

Introduction

A safari is a trip, a journey. You may wish to go on safari to discover something new. Or you may decide to go on safari to enjoy something that you have already experienced. The word *safari* comes from two words in the Swahili language, *Ar sofar,* which means "journey." Swahili is spoken by some groups of African people.

Travelers often go on safari to India or Africa. They hunt for lions, tigers, or other animals. These days people do not hunt these animals to kill them, but to watch them, and take their pictures.

You don't have to go to faraway jungles to find what is rare and unusual in nature. There is much that you can discover in your own backyard. Your yard may be a small one, or a large garden. Perhaps you live near a vacant lot in a city. Or you could be near a country road or a path through a park. The more often you explore any one place, the more you will discover.

Nothing in nature remains the same. As the earth keeps turning, everything changes. These changes are brought right to your door. Each day, each week, each season is different.

There are fifty-two weeks in a year. This book describes fifty-two safaris, one for each week. You can plan to go on safari every week. As the spinning planet travels around the sun, it will carry you along through all four seasons.

I wish you many pleasant and exciting journeys.

WINTER

* *
 *

W e live in the Northern Hemisphere. In this part of the world, we have four seasons each year. The reason for the different seasons is the way Planet Earth is tilted as it travels around the sun.

It takes the earth one year to circle completely around the sun. When the Northern Hemisphere is tilted so it is farthest from the sun, the days become shorter. Shorter days provide less sunshine, and, therefore, less heat. This means that winter, the coldest season of the year, is here.

Winter's cold temperatures bring ice and snow. People keep comfortable by heating their homes and by wearing warm clothing. Some avoid the cold altogether by going south for the winter.

Many animals migrate to the south at this time of year. They return north the following spring. Such travelers include bats, some insects, moose, elk, and many birds.

Among the animals that live in the north all year and remain active during the winter are squirrels, deer, and blue jays. The woodchuck is what we call a true hibernator. It digs into the ground and sleeps all winter. Bears and chipmunks, on the other hand, sleep only during the coldest part of this season.

Trees and other plants have to protect themselves in winter as well. Most lose their leaves. Flowers may be gone, but seeds are left behind. These will grow into new plants in spring. When warm days return, new leaves will grow from buds on trees and shrubs.

Winter safaris are great for exploring the cold world. Bundle up and step outside to find out about plants and animals in winter, about snow and ice, and about the air and sky.

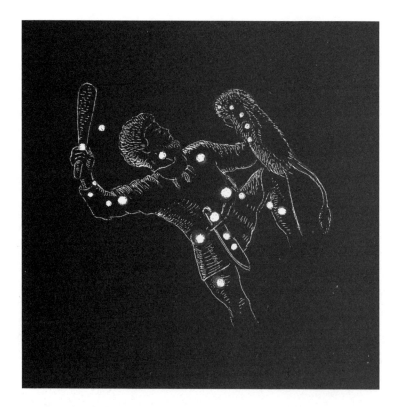

Find the Hunter in the Sky

It gets dark early in winter, and the night skies are often brilliant. The stars, which are actually faraway suns, shine like precious gems. Pick a clear winter night to bundle up and go outdoors to behold a star-spangled sky. The best time is about an hour after sunset.

Groups of bright stars form imaginary pictures. Such pictures are called constellations. One of the most famous winter constellations is the figure of Orion, the Hunter.

To locate Orion, first find the three stars that make up the hunter's belt. They resemble a short string of pearls. A mass of glowing gases seem to hang from his belt. You can imagine this to be his sword.

Several other stars make up this imaginary figure. A reddish, bright star is the right shoulder. This ruby looks even brighter when seen through a pair of field glasses. The star that shines like a blue-white diamond is where you would imagine Orion's left knee to be.

In this one constellation, Orion, you can find a fine collection of precious jewels.

Catch a Falling Snowflake

When snow is falling, tuck a magnifying glass in your pocket and go outside to look and listen. The snow is sparkling white and the snowflakes make no sound as they fall. Lift your face to the snow. Feel the flakes turn to water on your warm cheeks.

Hold out your arm to allow some snowflakes to land on your sleeve or mitten. The snowflakes will stand out more clearly if they land on a piece of velvet. You can pin a small piece of black velvet cloth to your sleeve for this purpose. If you don't have velvet, any piece of dark, rough cloth will do.

Look at the snowflakes through the magnifying glass. They appear much larger. Examine the exquisite designs of the tiny flakes of snow. Each flake is made of ice crystals, yet each is different.

Ice melts and snowflakes disappear. However, you can capture a snowflake and make it last by taking it indoors. You will need three things: Some glass slides, a piece of wood on which to spread out the slides, and a can of clear plastic spray. All of these must be *very* cold.

Lay the slides on the wood. Cover them lightly with a film of the plastic spray. Then hold the slides where some snow can fall on them. Next, take them to a cold place that is protected from the snow. Leave the snow-covered slides there to dry for about fifteen to twenty minutes.

The snowflakes will turn to plastic. You are now ready to examine them under a magnifying glass or a microscope. The plastic snowflakes can be kept practically forever. Keep them protected in a closed box. Mark the date of the snowfall on the box.

You can make a collection of plastic snowflakes from different years and from different times during a snowstorm. It will be interesting to compare them and a pleasure to admire them.

Living Specks on the Snow

Many different kinds of insects live on top of the snow. Snow insects are generally small and dark–little dots or specks on the snow. They often gather in large numbers, making them easier to find. One of the commonest kinds of snow insects is the snow flea. Snow fleas collect in huge crowds.

The snow flea can hop as well as walk. It walks with its six legs. It hops by means of a tiny leaping organ attached to the end of its body. This tailpiece is tucked up under its body, pointing forward. When the snow flea slaps its tailpiece down, the organ straightens out with a snap, tossing the insect into the air. The snow flea can spring 4 inches (10 centimeters) into the air. That's a big leap for such a tiny insect.

Snow fleas live underground or among damp fallen leaves on top of the soil. They feed on rotten wood or on other parts of decaying plant material. No one is sure why snow fleas appear above the snow in the winter. They may come above ground because they have run out of food and are searching for a new food supply.

A good time to look for snow insects is during a winter thaw. When the temperature is a little above freezing, you can find millions of them coming up through a crack in the snow. The white snow looks as if it has turned black where these insects march.

Animal Tracks

Whatever moves over the snow leaves its mark, so right after a light snowfall is the best time to try animal tracking. Although the tracks are visible, the track maker is usually not.

You can start by looking for tracks made by birds. Birds usually have four toes, three in front and one in back. Some birds hop and some walk.

Birds that hop land on the snow with both feet at the same time. Each hop leaves a pair of tracks. Sparrows hop. So do goldfinches, juncos, and robins.

If you see a single row of bird tracks, they belong to birds that walk. Pheasants, crows, starlings, and pigeons are walkers.

You can also find the footprints of four-legged animals. Squirrels, mice, and rabbits make pairs of tracks in sets of four; two hind feet and two front feet. They place their hind legs ahead of their front legs as they run.

Squirrels and mice have four toes on their front feet and five toes on their back feet.

Rabbits do not leave any toe prints because they have such

furry legs. Their hind legs make two long tracks followed by the two small, round ones of the front feet.

House cats and other members of the cat family, such as the bobcat, walk on their toe pads. Cats retract their claws when walking and leave a single file of round marks. There are no signs of toenails.

Dogs also walk on their toes but they cannot pull their claws in as cats do. Therefore, you can see the claw marks of dog tracks. Take your dog for a walk in the snow. Encourage the dog to walk, run, and leap. Then you can examine its snow tracks.

A walking dog leaves tracks that are close to each other. A running dog leaves sets of four tracks with long spaces between the sets. Fox tracks resemble dog tracks, but the fox walks in a single line. Dog tracks form a double line.

Deer walk on hooves. So do sheep, cows, and horses. A hoof is an enlarged toenail. Deer leave lines of large, heart-shaped tracks with a ridge in the center of each track.

Snow Puzzles

Awalk in the snow brings to mind many puzzling questions. For example, do you ever wonder what snow is made of? Think of what happens to snow when it melts. It turns to water. Snow is a form of water. If you melt cups of snow from different places and from different snowfalls, you will find that all snow is not the same. Each sample produces a different amount of water.

Find a snowdrift. Do you know what causes snowdrifts? When winds that carry snow die down, they drop their load of snow. This forms a wall of snow in the path of the wind called a snowdrift.

Why does snow around a tree melt faster than snow that lies a short distance away from the tree? The wood of the tree trunk gets warm from the sun. Then the heated wood melts the snow around the tree.

Why does the snow around a tree trunk melt in the form of an oval and not in the shape of a circle? Most sunlight falls on the south side of a tree. The south side of the trunk gets hotter. The north side gets the least amount of sun, so it heats up less than the other sides of the trunk. This uneven heating causes the snow to melt in the shape of an oval instead of a circle.

Why are snow fences built with spaces between the slats? Wind that carries snow is strong and powerful. The spaces allow the wind to go through, making its force less strong. This prevents the fence from being blown down.

Sometimes you see delicate circles etched on the snow. How are these made? When the wind blows tall grasses, they bend over, touching the snow and tracing dainty circles.

The snow, at times, looks as if someone has shaken black pepper over it. Each speck resembles a miniature bird. Do you know what the specks are? They are tiny plant scales that fall from birch tree catkins in the winter. If there is snow on the ground, the scales can be seen. They are called mimic birds because of their shape. The scales protect the tree's tiny seeds when they are packed in the catkins. The seeds also fall, but they are even smaller than the scales and very pale, so they are hard to see. You can see catkins hanging from birch trees throughout the winter.

These are a few of the many snow puzzles that may come to mind as you tramp through the snow. How many more snow puzzles can you think of?

Stories in the Snow

Animal tracks in the snow are clues. They tell you which animal made them, and by looking at them, you might even figure out what happened there. Many tales can be discovered from marks left in the snow.

The deer mouse, also called a white-footed mouse, often recycles an old bird nest by making it into a winter home. The mouse adds insulation for warmth. It also builds a roof to keep out rain and snow.

Deer mice make small tracks in sets of four. The paired tracks show the five-toed hind feet in front of the four-toed forefeet. Between the footprints is the drag mark of the tail.

Now hunt for deer mouse snow tracks that stop at the base of a tree. Can you see a bird's nest in the tree? It is seldom very high up. You can tell whether the deer mouse is at home if the snow is newly fallen and if there is only one row of tracks. The position of the front and back feet shows the direction in which the mouse traveled.

If the single trail leads away from the tree, you know that the deer mouse is not home. If the trail leads toward the tree,

chances are the deer mouse is home. Find a stick and knock on the tree trunk. You might find a little mouse's head with a pair of bright eyes peering at you.

Here is another story that is frequently revealed in the snow. Try to figure it out. Look for three clues in one spot: The empty shell of a sunflower seed or some other evidence of food, animal tracks, and a pair of wingmarks etched on the snow. What happened?

Marks in the snow do not last forever. They are erased when the snow melts or when new snow falls. Each new snowfall is followed by new tracks and new stories. This means new chances for more snow safaris.

The Sun's Energy at Work

Find some leaves that are lying on top of the snow. Some are dark and others light; some are small and others large. Most of the leaves lie in depressions below the surface of the snow. Some lie deeper down than others. How were the leaves pressed into the snow? They cannot dig down on their own. Nor do they sink down because of their weight. Leaves are not heavy enough.

You can perform a simple outdoor experiment to discover the answer to the puzzle. You will need five or six small metal disks, such as the tops of frozen-juice containers. Make sure that they are all the same size. After the disks are washed and well dried, paint one side of each one a different color. Be sure to include the colors black and white. The other colors can be whatever you choose. Let the disks dry.

Find a level surface on a patch of snow in the sunlight. Arrange the painted disks in a row on top of the snow. Place the white one first. The second one should be a little darker. The third one should be still darker, and so on. The black disk should be last. Let them lie in the sun for fifteen or twenty minutes.

When you return to the disks, notice that they have sunk. The longer they are exposed to the sunlight, the deeper they sink. Which disk has gone down deepest? You will find that the black metal is lower than the others. Each disk sinks to a different depth.

The sunlight strikes all the disks with an equal amount of light energy. The energy which is absorbed changes to heat energy. Heat causes the snow under each disk to melt. As the snow melts, the disk sinks down. Dark objects absorb more sunshine than lighter ones. The black disk absorbs the most. For this reason it heats up more than the others. This makes the most snow melt under the black disk.

The least amount of sunshine is absorbed by the white disk. White colors reflect most of the sunshine. The white disk heats up the least and it melts less snow than the others. This makes the white disk sink down less than the others.

Each color absorbs a different amount of sunlight. This makes the temperature of each disk different. Now you know why leaves sink down in the snow. You also know why the color of each leaf determines how deeply it will sink.

You may have noticed that black cars get hotter than white cars in the summertime. Suppose you were shopping for a warm winter jacket and you had a choice of colors. What color would you select if you wanted the warmest jacket?

19

A Safari to Eskimo Land

All you need is a good snowfall and you can pretend that you live in an igloo in the land of the Eskimos. Very few Eskimos live in snow igloos for more than a few days at a time. They usually build them when traveling.

The word *igloo* comes from the Eskimo word for house. When necessary, these people can build such a shelter out of snow in less than an hour. Using a special knife, they cut large bricks from packed snow. These bricks are arranged in a kind of circle.

When the igloo is finished, it looks like a large bowl turned upside down. A small entrance, which is dug underground, leads into the house. This is dug underground to keep out the wind and the cold. The igloo is nice and cozy inside. It may even get hot. The heat comes from lighted lamps and from body heat.

You can get an idea of how it feels to live in an igloo by building a snow house of your own. After a big snowfall, make a large, round pile of snow. The pile should be as tall as you are and about 5 feet (1.5 meters) across. Shovel out the inside, taking care not to break the walls. Make a small entrance, one that is just big enough for you to go in and out. You may wish to put a piece of plastic or some kind of ground cloth on the floor.

There are several things that you can find out about your igloo. When the sun is shining, compare the inside temperature with the outside temperature. Make the same comparison on a cloudy day. Does the heat of your body make a difference? Sit inside for a little while and record the temperature every five minutes. If the temperature rises, it is your body heat that supplies the warmth.

If there is room in your igloo, invite a friend to sit with you. Record the temperature every five minutes while the two of you are sharing the snow house. How much warmer does it get with two people inside instead of just one person?

Snow provides good insulation. It helps to keep the ground warm. Compare the temperatures taken in these three places: The air above a pile of snow, the snow in the middle of the pile, and the ground beneath the pile.

Can you find clues to animals and plants living under the snow? What part of your igloo melts first? Maybe you would like to write a poem about how it feels to live in a house made of snow. Think of other investigations that you could make while you are living as an Eskimo.

Hidden Wildlife

Goldenrod is one of the most common weeds in North America. It can be found just about everywhere. The yellow blossoms on the tall, green stalks appear late in summer. After the flowers bloom and form seeds, they lose their bright color. Their fluffy, darkened tops, holding thousands of goldenrod seeds, remain throughout the winter.

Storms and winds may toss the flower heads until they resemble small, torn rags. Many of the seeds are scattered to other places, where they will start new goldenrod plants the following spring. Some of the seeds nourish birds and small animals, such as field mice. What's most interesting is that some very small animals spend the winter safely hidden and protected within the goldenrod plant.

Go on safari to hunt for these creatures. The only equipment you will need is a magnifying glass. After you find a patch of goldenrod, examine the flower stalks. Look for stalks that have a bulge, or swelling, somewhere along the middle of the stem. The swelling, which is called a goldenrod ball gall, resembles a small, brown ball. There may be one or several such galls on one stalk.

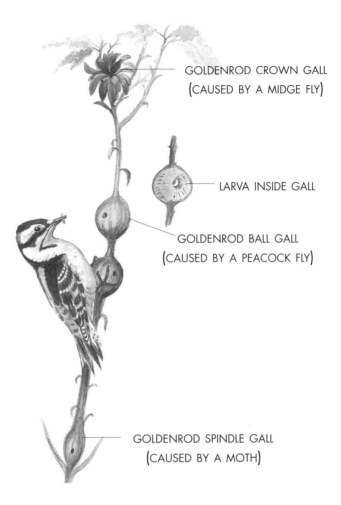

GOLDENROD CROWN GALL
(CAUSED BY A MIDGE FLY)

LARVA INSIDE GALL

GOLDENROD BALL GALL
(CAUSED BY A PEACOCK FLY)

GOLDENROD SPINDLE GALL
(CAUSED BY A MOTH)

Try to pry the ball gall open with your fingernails. If it is too tough for your nails, get an adult to help you with a small penknife. Look for a tiny, white animal inside. With a little twig, gently remove it onto your hand. A magnifying glass will help you to see its little ridges. It will probably move about in its strange environment. If you find one of these animals late in winter, you can take it home and put it in a little bottle with a small piece of moist paper. Cover the top of the bottle. Make a tiny opening in the top to give the animal some air. You may see it develop into an adult insect called a peacock fly.

How did the tiny insect get inside the flower stalk? The previous spring, an adult female peacock fly laid an egg on top of a goldenrod stalk. The egg hatched and a tiny wormlike animal came out. At this stage, it is called a larva. The larva began to eat and eat. It ate its way down the flower stalk and eventually stopped. The larva has a kind of built-in clock that tells it where and when to stop. The plant then developed the gall around the larva. This became the larva's winter home. Here it lived, ate, and grew until it finally turned into a little brown form. At this stage, it is called a pupa.

When the following spring arrives, the pupa goes through many changes. One day in March it turns into an adult peacock fly and leaves its winter home. At this time you can look for galls with tiny, round holes in them. These are the exit holes of the adult flies.

You may find a gall ball with a jagged opening as if someone tore it to get inside. This usually means that a downy woodpecker made a meal of the larva, as they frequently do. Ice fishermen claim that the grubs make excellent fish bait. Apparently you are not the only hunter on safari for this hidden wildlife.

"Stickers"

Y ou have seen how the goldenrod provides one kind of wildlife adventure. There are still more kinds to be found in other common weeds. After a day outdoors at this time of year, you are apt to come home with a variety of seeds sticking to your clothes. Your dog may often appear with a seed collection sticking to its coat as well. If you examine the seeds, you will find that they have either small or large spines. The spines enable the seeds to hitch a ride on the fur of animals or on people's clothing. When the seeds fall or are brushed off, they may start to grow the following spring. This is one way in which plants spread from one location to another.

One of the most interesting hitchhikers is commonly called sticker. Stickers are the burs, or fruits, of the weed burdock. Each sticker is an entire flower head of seeds. Burdock can be found easily in city lots and just about everywhere in the country.

Examine the stickers with a magnifying glass to find the little hooks that catch onto things. You can also see the hooks with your naked eye and feel them with your fingers. It is said that when a man named Mr. Velcro saw these little, hooked spines, he was inspired to design the Velcro fastener.

Remove one sticker from a burdock plant. Pry it open with your fingers. Some of the seeds will separate easily. If you come across a clump that is hard to separate, you have probably found the winter home of a little wild animal. Keep trying until you separate some of the seeds in the clump.

If some of the plant spines stick on your skin, remove them by putting a piece of masking tape over the spines and peeling it off. The spines will cling to the tape.

Once the clump is open, look inside for a fat, little grub with a golden head. The grub, also called a larva, will emerge as an adult moth in the spring. Meanwhile it feeds on the nourishment stored in the burdock.

Count the number of stickers on one burdock plant. Each sticker bears a large number of seeds. You may count the number of seeds on several stickers and you will know approximately how many seeds are on each little fruit head. If you multiply that number by the number of fruit heads, you will get an idea of how many seeds there are in one burdock plant. It has been estimated that one plant may bear as many as forty thousand seeds. These seeds could easily provide winter homes for some thirty thousand little moth larvae. You probably never guessed that the stickers of the common burdock provide winter homes for such a large wildlife population.

BURDOCK PLANT

GOLDEN-HEADED
LARVA OF MOTH

CROSS SECTION OF
BURDOCK STICKER

Owl Pellets

Owls are meat eaters. They search mostly for mice and other small animals. Some owls also feed on small birds. Whatever prey they catch, they swallow it whole in one gulp.

Owls hunt at night and rest during the day. They digest their food while resting. All parts of the prey are broken down except fur and bones. These undigested parts are rolled up into a pellet which the owl then coughs up and spits out. An owl may cough up two to four pellets a night.

If you find some owl pellets on the ground, look for owls in the trees above. You have found trees that some owls have selected as their roosting place. Pellets are also found in and around barns. It is not unusual to find owl pellets at the bases of trees in cities as well, especially in city parks. Where you find pellets, you can look for the owls that produced them.

Collect a few pellets and take them apart. You can find out what the owls eat and what animals live in the neighborhood. Each kind of owl produces pellets of a different shape, color, and size. Pellets may be round or oval, smooth or bumpy, shiny or dull. They may be black, gray, or tan, and small, medium, or

OWL PELLET

large. A barn owl pellet may be 2 inches (5 centimeters) long, while a little owl's pellet is only 1 inch (2.5 centimeters) long.

Pellets are clean and easy to separate. You can use two small twigs to tease them apart, or you can use your fingers. Look for little bones, teeth, jaws, and skulls packed into the fur. It is best to work over a piece of paper so that you do not lose any of the tiny parts.

Some farmers spray their fields in order to destroy undesirable plants. How could this spraying affect the owls? Why should the farmer consider owls to be helpful animals?

Artistic Beetles

A safari to your own backyard can turn into an interesting art show. All you need is an elm tree or a woodpile where you may find some elm logs.

The American elm was once one of our most common trees. Its shape is very graceful, somewhat like a tall flower vase. The way the branches form an arch overhead makes it a perfect shade tree. For many years it was one of the most frequently planted shade trees. Rows of elms provided relief from the sun for city dwellers, while elms on farms sheltered cattle. Elms were also planted in parks and in backyards.

About seventy years ago, our elms began to die. This happened when some logs infected with Dutch elm disease were accidentally shipped from Europe to the United States. Thousands of American elms contracted the illness and died. Many are still dying, although a few seem to be surviving. Scientists have now developed a new elm, called the American Liberty elm. This elm is resistant to the Dutch elm disease.

This disease is caused by a fungus. There are many kinds of fungi. Fungi reproduce by tiny cells called spores. The spores that cause Dutch elm disease are spread by Dutch elm beetles when the beetles fly from sick to healthy elm trees.

When a spore falls on a healthy elm, the spore grows and develops into a branching fungus. The fungus grows rapidly, clogging the water and food canals inside the tree. As a result, the tree is unable to continue making its own food. It becomes ill and dies.

The Dutch elm beetle is also called a bark beetle because it spends part of its life under the bark of trees. While the beetle lives and feeds under the bark, it makes curious designs. These designs can be seen on the bare trunk and on the inside pieces of loose bark that hang from sick elm trees. You can often find loose bark on the ground beneath the trees.

Look at the bare wood under the bark. Some of the designs may look like centipedes crawling up the tree trunk. These designs are made when the female Dutch elm beetle is ready to lay her eggs. Finding a sick elm with loose bark, she crawls under the bark and digs a little groove straight up and down. The groove is about 1.5 inches (4 centimeters) long.

The beetle lays its row of eggs in this shallow ditch. When the eggs hatch, each little wormlike larva digs its own feeding gallery out from the main ditch. The collection of feeding galleries resemble the many legs coming out of a centipede's body. When the larvae become adult beetles, they leave the sick elm and fly to a healthy elm to feed. Many of the Dutch elm beetles brush against the fungus spores as they leave the sick trees. When the beetles arrive to feed on healthy elms, some of the spores drop off from their bodies and land on the elms.

There is also an American elm beetle whose life-style is similar to that of the Dutch elm beetle. It makes the same kind of design, with one difference. The female American elm beetle

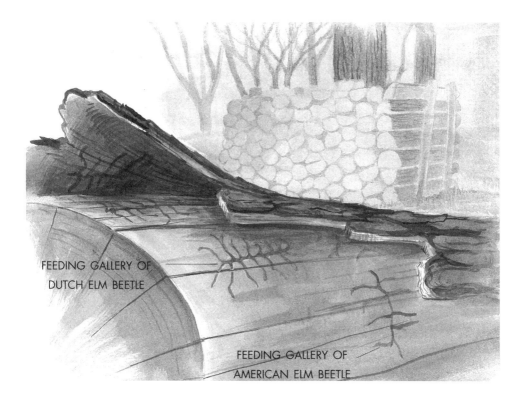

FEEDING GALLERY OF
DUTCH ELM BEETLE

FEEDING GALLERY OF
AMERICAN ELM BEETLE

digs a horizontal ditch in which she lays her eggs. Her finished design looks like a centipede crawling around the tree, rather than up and down it.

Because elm wood makes excellent firewood, a woodpile is another good place to search for logs with the designs of these engraver beetles. While you are examining the barks of trees, you will probably come across many different markings on the tree trunks.

Each kind is made by a different type of insect. Did you ever think you could find an art exhibit on the wood of a sick elm tree?

Winter Activity at the Bird Feeder

A great many things go on at a bird feeder in the winter. Take a safari to one or more bird feeders in your neighborhood. Most of the activity takes place in the early morning, at noon, and again at about four o'clock in the afternoon. Stand still and watch what is happening. The birds that fly off when you arrive will soon return to feed. Birds require a lot of energy to keep warm at this time of year. Their food provides them with the energy they require.

Listen to the bird sounds. Birds are forever chattering. They have their own language, and each sound has a special meaning for other birds. If a blue jay spots a cat or a hawk, it utters a scream that sounds as if it is saying, "Thief! Thief!" This is a signal to other birds to fly away or "freeze." Jays are often called the policemen of the woods.

The constant chatter among birds at a feeder informs passing birds that there is food to be had at this spot. Many accept the invitation.

Some birds feed very peacefully. For example, finches seem to get along with one another quite nicely. However, there are birds like the blue jays, who are forever pushing and shoving. What kind of "table manners" do you observe at the feeder?

Look for crows, sparrows, cardinals, and juncos on the ground. They are chiefly ground feeders. The cardinal will also visit the feeder. The crow might try to do the same. Chickadees, nuthatches, goldfinches, and other small birds get their nourishment at the feeder.

Different birds have different feeding habits. Watch a chickadee grab a seed. It flies to the branch of a tree and eats all alone. It cracks the seed open with its beak while holding on to the seed with its feet. At the same time it has to balance itself on the tree. Chickadees are fast feeders. Notice how frequently they fly to and fro.

Blue jays are big eaters. After gulping down a bunch of seeds, a blue jay fills its gullet with another load of seeds and flies off to a tree. Here it pushes the seeds into cracks, storing them for future use. It is interesting to watch each kind of bird for a long time to learn its habits.

You can become part of the action at a feeder. Place some sunflower seeds in your open hand. Stand very still and stretch out your arm while holding up the seeds. Be patient. In time, a chickadee may accept your offer. It may grab a seed and be off, but it should return again and again. The feel of half an ounce of fluff on your hand is one of the greatest outdoor thrills.

Looking and listening at the feeder is a good way to learn about all kinds of wildlife. You will see more than birds. Squirrels, deer, and many other animals are attracted by the food. Besides, feeder watching is great fun.

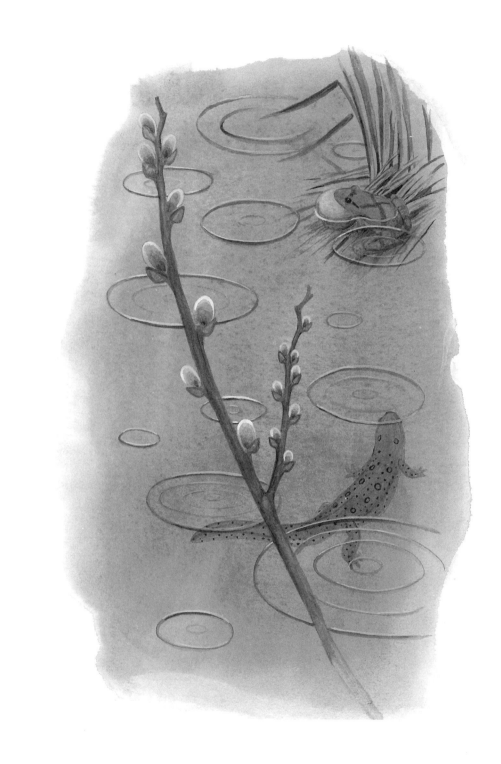

SPRING

We eagerly await spring. Spring means warm weather. On about March 21, spring finally arrives. The days have been getting longer, and on the first day of spring, night and day are of equal lengths. Each is twelve hours long. From then on, for thirteen weeks, the days continue to lengthen, while the nights become shorter. We soon realize, however, that the first day of spring is not the first spring day–it could be cold and windy. But warm days will eventually arrive–glorious, sunny spring days.

Longer periods of sunlight warm the earth, and spring rains moisten the earth. This makes for many changes. Seeds sprout and plants grow. Birds, butterflies, and insects return to this new green world. Ponds and streams become lively with fish, frogs, salamanders, and turtles. You will find something to discover outside wherever you look.

For the next three months, you can go outdoors and enjoy all sorts of new spring adventures.

Life Underground—Earthworms

Look for little holes that suddenly appear in the soil in late March or early April. The holes are about the thickness of a pencil. A small pile of little earth balls surrounds every hole. Each of these openings leads into an earthworm's home, an underground burrow.

During the winter, the earthworms collected in bunches down in the soil below the frost line. They lived on the food stored in their bodies. As the soil warmed up, they separated, and each worm ate its way up through the earth. When the worms reached the surface, they fed and found mates.

The collection of little earth balls surrounding an earthworm's burrow is rich in minerals. The balls, called castings, were formed as the worms ate their way to the top of the soil.

Earthworms are important animals because they turn over huge amounts of soil each year. It is estimated that rich soil may have as many as one million earthworms living in each acre. This means that they may move as much as thirty-five tons of plants and soil in one year. In this way, the worms help to fertilize the soil naturally. In addition, their burrows admit air and water to the soil.

Earthworms feed mostly at night. Fishermen, who use the worms for bait, call them night crawlers. The worms come part way out of their burrows to feed. The bottom part of the worm holds on to the inside of its burrow, while the top part moves around and searches for bits of fresh or decayed plants. The earthworm pulls the food down into its burrow to eat. Earthworms are flexible creatures. Watch a robin nab an earthworm. Sometimes there is a real tug-of-war as the bird pulls at its victim.

A good time to go on safari in search of earthworms is on a cloudy or rainy day. Earthworms breathe through their skin. When it rains and their burrows fill with water, the worms come out to keep from drowning. They are sensitive to light and noise. Watch them retreat when you stamp your foot near them. What happens if you turn a flashlight on them?

Earthworms are only part of the wildlife to be found in the soil. A little careful digging could reveal many more organisms whose homes are underground.

Skunk Cabbage—Spring's First Wildflower

Go on safari to a wet area if you wish to find the first spring blossom. The ground may still be a little frozen, and there may even be some snow on the ground. Still, you might see the colorful hood of the skunk cabbage poking up through the cold. The pointed green, brown, and purple hood shelters the little flowers inside.

Both the male and female flowers grow on a short, stout structure under the protective hood. The flowers warm up as they develop. Most of the heat is produced as the eggs and pollen are being formed. The temperature under the hood may go up to 72°F (22°C). This is warm enough to melt a path up through the frozen earth.

The warmth and nourishment that is provided by the skunk cabbage at this time of year attracts bees and flies in search of an early spring meal. Flies are attracted by the color of the hood, which resembles meat, as well as by the odor of the plant, which smells like decayed flesh. Flies lay their eggs on decaying meat.

As the flowers continue to develop, large, bright green leaves appear. The plant is beautiful in spite of its odor. Appreciate it as a humble messenger who announces, "Spring is here."

Horsetails–Leftover Plants
from Ancient Times

Look at any flower and you will see a busy seed factory. While the flower is blooming, seeds are being manufactured inside of it. The blossom fades when the seeds are ripe. Next year's blossoms will grow from these new seeds.

Not all plants have flowers, although they all have a way of reproducing themselves. The plants called horsetails are among the most interesting nonflowering plants. Horsetails grow in many backyards and fields, as well as along roads and railroad tracks. The two most common horsetails are the field horsetail and the scouring rush.

The field horsetail has two kinds of stems which grow up from an underground part of the plant. A tan, 6-inch (15-centimeter) jointed stem appears very early in spring. The stem has a collar of tiny, dark leaves at each joint and resembles a small, pale asparagus stalk. A beautiful cone develops on top of the stalk. The cone is made up of little spore cases. Each case is packed full of tiny spores. If you shake some spores on your hand, it looks like greenish talcum powder.

Spores do for nonflowering plants what seeds do for flowering plants. When the ripe spores of horsetails scatter, they form

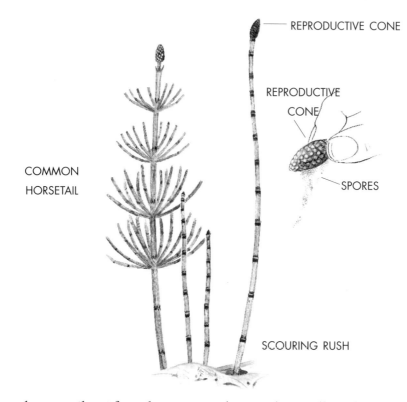

REPRODUCTIVE CONE

REPRODUCTIVE
CONE

COMMON
HORSETAIL

SPORES

SCOURING RUSH

new horsetails. After the spores leave the stalks, the entire stem dies down. Its work is done, and another kind of stalk grows up from below.

This second stem grows taller and is colored green. Narrow, green, needlelike leaves grow out from each of its joints. This arrangement has been compared to a neatly tied horse's tail, which is how the plant originally got its name.

Scouring rush, the other common horsetail, has tall, hollow, green jointed stalks. The little cones with the spore cases are on the tops of the stalks.

Both the field horsetail and the scouring rush have sand in their tissues. You can feel the roughness if you bite into a piece of plant stalk. Horsetails, especially the scouring rush, have been used from the earliest times as a natural sandpaper. People used the stalks to scrub pots and pans. Some campers still do. Break up some horsetails at the joints and make a little bundle of them. Use this to scrub a dull copper penny until it shines. You will find this easy to do.

The ancestors of horsetails lived on this planet millions of years ago. They resembled modern plants in everything but size, for the ancient horsetails were huge trees that grew in swamps. When they died and were pressed into the earth, they changed, gradually turning into coal. When we burn coal, the energy that has been locked up in those old trees provides us with heat. This energy originally came from the sunshine during prehistoric times when the leaves of the trees were manufacturing food. That is why coal is called a fossil fuel and is said to store fossil sunshine.

When you go on safari in search of horsetails, you will find small, modern relatives of the ancient giants from the coal age.

ANCIENT SWAMP

Housecleaning Ants

There are about three thousand different kinds of ants. You can easily observe one kind, known as the pavement or sidewalk ant. These ants build their homes in the soil under stones. Look for them along roadsides, at the edges of driveways, in cracks in driveways, and near large stones. They are also found between the cracks of city sidewalks. The pavement ant is a European immigrant that established itself in this country.

A colony of these ants consists of a queen, numerous larvae, or immature ants, and a great many strong worker ants. The males that fertilize the eggs of the queen die soon after their job is done. The workers take care of the large, underground ant colony.

Some guard the nest, while others provide food. One of the most interesting jobs performed by the workers is housecleaning. By cleaning, they ventilate the nest.

Look for small piles of sand or soil heaped up around little holes in the ground. Each hole is an entrance to an ant nest. Keep your eye on the hole and watch for worker ants coming up from below. Each carries a grain of sand or soil in its mouth. As the worker pops out of the hole, it immediately drops its load, turns around, and disappears down the hole again. Soon it appears with another load. This goes on all day, every day, until late afternoon. The ants are warming and drying the soil that they bring up from below. Notice that their work is going on in the warm sunshine. The pile may reach 2 inches (5 centimeters) across and 0.5 inch (over 1 centimeter) high before the workers stop coming up.

The workers seem to know when the sand grains are warm and dry. In the late afternoon, they reverse their march, carrying the aired grains of soil or sand back down into the nest. This possibly provides the colony with a comfortable night's rest. Imagine having such a housecleaning job as a life assignment!

Return of the Robins

Early spring may still be quite cold. But even if the temperature rises a few degrees above freezing, it is time to look for the return of the robins. Some robins may have remained in your area throughout the winter, but most of them flew south. The new spring arrivals come in flocks, settle on the ground, and search for something to eat. Notice that these early birds are all males. A male robin has a brick red breast and a black head.

At first the males are silent, but after a few days, they start their regular serenades. They sing early in the morning and surprisingly late in the evening. Some people imagine that the birds sing, "Cheerily, cheerily, cheer up." You may interpret the song in any way that pleases you.

About a week after the males arrive, the females join them. The female robin's breast is not as bright as the male's, and her head is gray. Robins return to the same territory each year.

The males and females pair off and look for nesting places. Robins often build around homes. They may select a site on a windowsill, a ledge, above an outdoor lamp, or in a nearby tree. The female does the building. The male supplies her with the materials.

Watch what the male carries in his beak. You may observe him carrying grass, plant stalks, bits of string, pieces of paper, snips of fabric, and other such materials. The outside of the nest may look untidy, but the inside is very smooth. The nest is lined with soft grass and mud. Before the mud hardens, the female robin fixes the inside of the nest so it will fit her shape.

When the nest is finished and the female is ready, she will lay her first clutch of four eggs. The eggs are a beautiful blue color and have to be kept warm for about two weeks. This is mostly the job of the female. The male may relieve her now and then, but only for a little while. After this period, which is called incubation, the eggs hatch. The babies remain in the nest for about another two weeks. Both parents work hard to feed the hungry babies. At this stage the young eat mostly animal food, such as earthworms and caterpillars. The male continues to feed the young even as the female begins to build a nest for her second brood.

There is a great deal to observe in the life of a robin. You can get to know them as individuals. One robin's song could be quite different from another's, even though it still sounds like a typical robin song. A robin has more than just one song. You can find out what the others are and when the robin sings each kind. You can also discover other things about robins: What foods do they eat? Who are their enemies? How many robin nests can you find in a given area? Do robins behave gently, or are they quarrelsome?

Many other birds arrive in the spring. Another early bird is the bluebird. Listen as it whistles, "Purity, purity." The bluebird has the color of the sky on its back and the earth on its breast. Perhaps next year you will wish to concentrate on the bluebird.

You can go on two kinds of bird safaris. One kind is to investigate one bird's life in detail. A second kind is to learn to recognize all the birds in your neighborhood. In this case, a book on birds would be of great help. Whatever type of bird safari you choose, you are sure to have lots of fun.

A Pixy in a Violet

Violets are as welcome as springtime. They are called shy flowers because they are small. Although they are little, violets are both beautiful and interesting. Sit down near a group of violets. You may recognize the flowers by their violet, or purple, color. However, there are also yellow, white, and many-colored violets. Most of them have heart-shaped leaves.

Each flower has five petals. The lowest petal is larger than the other four petals. Look for little marks on this petal. These are guidelines that direct visiting insects to a little sac at the base of the petal near the stem. This sac, called the spur, is a storage place for the sweet nectar that bees use to make honey and that other insects also enjoy. There are five stamens in the violet. Stamens produce pollen. Two of the five stamens are different. They manufacture nectar. You can find these two stamens bent backward into the little spur.

There is an old story about pixies and violets. It is told that pixies, sometimes called fairies, dance all night. At dawn, when their tiny feet are very tired, each pixy finds a violet in which to rest during the day. If you would like to see one of the pixies, pick a violet. Carefully peel off the violet's largest petal. You will find the pixy resting on her throne with a golden crown on her head. Her two tiny feet are in the tub of nectar. She is taking a footbath. Her feet are the two bent stamens.

You can also find pixies taking footbaths in both wild and cultivated pansies. Wild pansies are also called Johnny-jump-ups. They pop up in gardens, backyards, and battlefields, which is how they got their name. These wildflowers are the ancestors of the cultivated pansies that people plant in their gardens. While on safari looking for violets, you may come across their relatives, the pansies. All have the same design. Find the largest of the five petals and look for the fairies living within.

Spring Butterflies

Most butterflies do not spend the winter as adults but as eggs, wormlike larvae, or quiet pupae. There are two exceptions. The large, orange and black monarch butterflies migrate as adults to warmer climates closer to the equator. The mourning cloak butterflies remain in North America all winter, also as adults.

The mourning cloak is a welcome sign of spring. It hibernates during the cold weather in the crack of a tree or in a pile of stones or wood. As soon as there is a break in the weather, it is time to look for this butterfly. There may yet be some snow on the ground, but a warm day in early spring is butterfly safari time.

The mourning cloak has dark, purplish brown wings. The wings have a broad yellow edge with a row of pale blue dots. The only food available at this time of year is tree sap dripping from a broken twig or branch. Sometimes several mourning cloaks will gather in one spot to feed.

Another early butterfly is called the spring azure. It is small, blue, and beautiful. It looks like a delicate blue flower in flight.

Soon, white cabbage butterflies and yellow sulphur butterflies arrive. The whites lay their eggs on cabbages. The sulphurs are

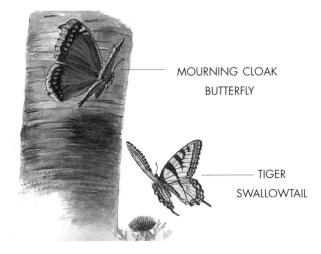

MOURNING CLOAK
BUTTERFLY

TIGER
SWALLOWTAIL

named for their yellow color. Sulphurs fly low, searching for water on the ground.

In June you may come across tiger swallowtails joining the mud puddlers. These swallowtails are strong flyers. They are bright yellow with black stripes, the same coloring that tigers have.

The butterflies seek their mates. When the female is ready to lay her eggs, she searches for a plant or tree that will provide just the right food for her young and lays her eggs on its leaves. When the eggs hatch, the larvae, called caterpillars, feed on the leaves. They have strong mouth parts at this stage and sometimes damage the plant on which they are feeding.

Following this larval stage, the caterpillar enters a quiet period called the pupal stage and changes into a pupa. The pupa is wrapped up in a protective covering called a chrysalis. It is in this chrysalis that the adult develops. When the right time comes, the adult breaks through the chrysalis, and the butterfly emerges. After a while, when its wings are stretched and dried, the butterfly flies off.

Butterfly watching is a delightful pastime from spring into summer.

Spring Peepers

Spring arrives with many different sights and sounds. Fat, silvery pink "pussies" on the pussy willows are a familiar sign of early spring. This is a good time to go on safari to a wet area, such as a pond, a bog, or a depression in the ground where melting snow makes a temporary pool.

Listen for the sweet chorus of "peep, peep, peep" coming from a watery place. This is the song of the tree frogs called spring peepers. Spring peepers are hard to find in the daytime. They seem to be absolutely invisible and stop calling as soon as you approach.

Spring peepers are small, barely 1 inch (2.5 centimeters) long, and usually hide among the damp mosses and leaves where they spent the winter. Their coloring blends right into the background. They are brown with a darker brown Greek cross on their backs. It is much easier to find the peepers at night. They do not seem to mind the light from flashlights or lanterns.

These animals do not open their mouths when they sing. Air expelled forcefully from their lungs passes across their vocal cords, making the cords move back and forth, or vibrate. These vibrations produce the sound.

Singing is the male spring peeper's way of seeking a mate and claiming his territory. The eggs are laid by the females during mating. They are deposited one at a time or in small masses of four to ten eggs. Look for their tiny eggs in April on the bottom of a pond or on plants.

Daytime singing stops around the middle of April, but the male peepers continue to sing at night, with their musical chorus lasting from dusk to dawn. By early May, most of the singing stops. However, some individual peepers continue to sing during the night all through summer and even as late as November.

Toads–like their relatives, the spring peepers–also sing. The song of the American toad is a beautiful trill. Its lovely serenade can be heard both day and night. When they hear this song, many people think it belongs to a bird.

INFLATED THROAT SAC OF
SINGING SPRING PEEPER

Dandelions–the Dandy "Lions"

Dandelions are among the most abundant, useful, and beautiful plants. They are also quite amazing. They grow all over the world, including our backyards, gardens, fields, and roadsides. They are found in poor soil and in rich soil, in the bright sunshine and in partial shade. Dandelions can be found blossoming every month of the year, but their flowers are most abundant during the early half of May.

As you step outside one sunny May morning, it looks as if your world is filled with dandelions–little disks of golden sunshine. Nobody minds if you pick dandelions. Pick a few and enjoy their delightful fragrance. Look at the leaves with their jagged edges. It was once suggested that their shape resembled the jaw of a lion. That was how the dandelion got its name. In France, the flower is called *dent de lion,* or "lion's tooth." When it originally came to this country from Europe, its name came along with it.

Now examine the yellow flowers. A dandelion is not one blossom; it is a collection of blossoms. Each yellow part is not a petal, but a complete little flower called a floret. When you hold one dandelion, you are really holding an entire bouquet of flowers.

Each floret produces one little fruit with a single dandelion seed. One flower head holds about two hundred florets, which can result in about two hundred seeds. Each dandelion plant may develop ten heads in a season. You can figure out how many dandelion seeds this means for next season–and all from one plant!

One day the dandelion flowers are gone. They are replaced by a mass of gray, fluffy balls. These are the dandelion fruits. Blow on one of these "blow balls" and watch the little parachutes sail away. Each has a tiny seed attached to it. When the wind scatters the fruits with their seeds, they fall with their pointed ends down. Where the seeds land on soil and are watered by rain, a new plant may grow.

Remove the head of dandelion flowers or fruits and you are left with a hollow stem that is narrower at the top end. You can push the narrow end of the stalk into the wider end to make a ring. From this you can make a chain of rings and fashion a necklace or a crown.

Would you like to paint a picture of a dandelion? Sketch an outline of the flower on a piece of paper. Remove a flower head. Squeeze it flat from side to side so you can use it as a paintbrush. Now paint the picture. Dandelions produce a bright yellow dye. Paint the leaves green with the dandelion leaves.

You can also eat dandelions. Young leaves are used for salads and in sandwiches. They are rich in Vitamins A and C. The leaves can also be cooked as a vegetable. The flowers are used for making jelly and wine. The roasted roots are ground up to make a dandelion coffee drink.

Perhaps the most fun, though, is to collect a dandelion bouquet, because then you are gathering a bunch of sunshine.

A Nighttime Spring Safari

Anighttime safari can be an exciting adventure, and you don't have to go far. Your own backyard will become a strange and mysterious place at night. It will look, feel, sound, and smell very different from what you experience by day.

Provide yourself with a comfortable seat. Now locate where west is. West is where the sun sets. Notice that night does not fall, but rises up as the darkness grows.

As it gets darker, your pupils get larger, thus admitting more light to your eyes. In less than an hour, you will become so used to the dark that you will be able to see as well as an owl and better than a rabbit. Your hearing will become sharper. You may discover sounds, songs, squeaks, and creaks made by birds, other animals, trees, and insects.

Notice that Orion, the Hunter, is sinking below the skyline. Soon this winter constellation will disappear. Leo, the Lion, is the new constellation for spring.

Listen for unfamiliar night sounds. Can you hear the trill of the American toad or the song of the spring peeper? The calls of spring peepers travel great distances. Cup your hands behind your ears to hear them more loudly. The sound, which resembles the jingling of sleigh bells, can be almost deafening.

If you can get to a pond, take a flashlight with you. Put a piece of clear red cellophane over the light. While night animals may be sensitive to dim light and movement, they are not bothered by red light. Now you can observe beavers, muskrats, frogs, or whatever comes your way. Night is full of new experiences.

Once There Was a Tree

Let's explore a dead tree. Of course all dead trees were once alive. Dead or alive, a tree is never alone. Living trees attract birds, insects, squirrels, and other animals and provide them with food and a place to live. They also attract other plants. Their trunks may be decorated with patches of plants, called lichens, in gold, gray, green, or yellow. Early in the spring, before the new leaves of the tree cast a heavy shadow, you may find the ground beneath them filled with a variety of wildflowers.

Eventually all trees die. Some kinds live only about twenty-five years. Others live longer, even hundreds of years. Many trees die young because they are injured. They may be damaged by disease, or automobiles, storms, or other accidents. Even after a tree dies, it may remain standing for a long time. Even then, it always has company.

Many kinds of insects live in dead trees. Wood-boring beetles make small holes in the bark. Carpenter ants tunnel through the wood in search of the beetles. As the dead tree decays, it becomes soft and grows weaker. Now it attracts other kinds of living things. Each kind will either make or use a hole of a different size. How many different sizes of holes can you find?

The downy woodpecker may find a hole that is just right for its nest. If the wood is soft enough, larger woodpeckers may chip out a larger nesting hole. Sometimes a branch breaks and leaves behind an opening with space enough inside for a flying squirrel or a screech owl. A large hole in a dead tree is often home for a family of raccoons.

The holes in a dead tree increase in size and number until the tree becomes too weak to stand. A storm or a strong wind may knock it over. Then the fallen tree becomes a log. Many different kinds of living things are attracted to the log, just as they were to the tree. Where the tree's roots were once in the ground, there is now a pit. A fox may choose to make its den in the pit. When the trunk becomes hollow, a skunk may move in.

Rain wets the log and the soil around it. This attracts salamanders, snakes, frogs, and toads. These animals move underneath the log where it is cool and moist.

Rain also softens the log, causing it to rot. Lift the rotting bark to find little gray sow bugs, centipedes, and slugs. Look for fuzzy patches of moss growing on top of the moist bark. Look for ferns there, too. The top of the log may soon look like a garden.

Reach inside and take a handful of rotting tree. It is very soft, brown, and crumbly, and has a good, earthy smell. Gradually, the whole tree turns to soil. A decayed tree forms rich soil. Look for tree seeds on and around the crumbling log. Perhaps some of them have already started to grow into new trees. The log, once a mighty tree, continues to live. It lives again as part of the new plants that it supports.

On Safari in the Rain

It is great sport to go on safari in the rain. Put on your boots and slicker, step outside, and you are ready for adventure. Sniff the air. It smells fresh and clean. Lift your face to the raindrops. Open your mouth and taste the rain. All your senses can enjoy a rainfall.

How did the rain get up in the sky, and what makes it fall down? When the sun shines, water evaporates from birdbaths, fountains, pools, puddles, rivers, and oceans. A great deal also evaporates from plants. Water evaporates in the form of an invisible gas. It rises high in the air, cools, and forms clouds. Clouds are made up of drops of water. When the drops are heavy enough, they fall as rain.

Look at the raindrops. How big are they? Are they all the same size? Here is an easy way to find out. Fill a pie pan with about half an inch (a little over a centimeter) of flour. Hold the pan out in the rain for a few seconds. Then take it indoors and let the flour dry for an hour or so. Notice the little, hard flour balls that were formed by the raindrops. Each flour ball is the size of the raindrop from which it was formed. Sift the flour from the pan

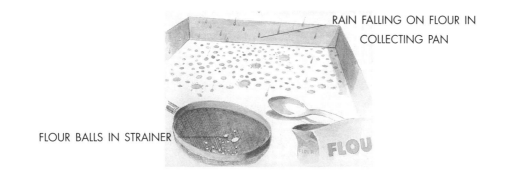

RAIN FALLING ON FLOUR IN COLLECTING PAN

FLOUR BALLS IN STRAINER

through a strainer onto a piece of paper. Sort the balls that remain in the strainer according to size. You may measure their exact size if you wish.

Have you ever seen a rainbow? It's a great thrill. To see one, go on safari in the morning or late afternoon on a rainy day when the sun is just coming out. The sun must be just right, not too high or too low. Stand with the sun on your back, looking straight ahead. As the white sunlight passes through the raindrops, it is broken up into the seven colors of the rainbow. Red is on the top, and violet is on the bottom. The other colors are in between.

You can also see a rainbow when the sunshine falls on the spray of a fountain or water hose. If you have a water hose with an adjustable nozzle, you can turn on the fine spray and try to make a rainbow of your own. Of course, you must have sunshine and rain at the same time. Remember to stand with the sun on your back.

When William Wordsworth, a famous poet, once saw a rainbow, he wrote a beautiful poem about it. These well-known lines are from that poem:

My heart leaps up when I behold
A rainbow in the sky. . . .

Turtletime

Springtime is also turtletime. Some turtles have been buried in the mud at the bottom of the water all winter long. When April arrives, the turtles receive a signal from inside their bodies that their hibernation is over. They awaken from their winter sleep and swim up into the sunshine.

There are many different kinds of turtles, but the most common one is the painted turtle. It is also one of the most beautiful. It has a smooth, dark green shell on top with red along the edge. The turtle's bottom shell is bright yellow. The neck and tail have both yellow and red markings. It *does* look as if someone had painted it.

Look for turtles on a sunny day at the edge of a pond or slow stream. You can also see them on a stone or on a log that is partly in the water. A common and amusing sight is a row of painted turtles crowded together on a log. If there is little room, they simply climb on top of one another in order to rest and warm themselves in the sunshine. As you approach, they suddenly dive into the water. However, if you stand quietly, they will return to continue their sunbathing.

The turtles remain in or near the water for food and safety. They feed on small water plants and water animals, such as snails and insects.

Painted turtles lay their eggs in the summer around the middle of July. Only the female leaves the water for dry land, when she is ready to make a nest and lay her eggs. This is a dangerous time for her. Turtles know nothing about automobiles. They are often seen crossing the road in their search for a suitable nesting place on dry land. Unfortunately, many are hit and killed.

The turtle's nest is a simple affair. The female scoops out a depression in the soil with her back feet, lays about ten eggs, and protects them by covering them with soil. Turtle mothers pay no further attention to their offspring. They return to the water for food, safety, and sunshine.

Several weeks later the baby turtles hatch and are on their own. They will try to find their way to a pond or stream. Many do not make it. Baby turtles are hard to find in the wild, but if you should see one, do not take it home. They are more apt to survive outdoors.

SUMMER

Summer means long, hot days. Shorter nights make it seem as if daytime is forever. It's a great season to have new experiences, and a wonderful time to go on many safaris. Summer is full of new sights, sounds, smells, tastes, and feelings.

Get up early one day, before the sun rises. Go outdoors and enjoy the feel of a summer dawn. Although the day may become hot, dawn feels cool and springlike, misty and fresh–a lovely way to start a day.

During the day, watch for hawks circling overhead as they search for prey. At such times crows often gather and noisily chase the hawks. The two appear to be born enemies.

Enjoy the pleasure of seeing summer butterflies, newly opened flowers, baby deer, baby birds, and many other new lives.

Listen to the special summer sounds. The buzzing sounds of cicadas, from high in the tops of trees, say it is summer. The sound starts off with a loud, fast buzzing, then slows down to a stop. Another seasonal sound is the bass call of the American bullfrog, our largest frog. From the pond you hear it call, "Jug-o-rum." Birds sing, katydids make their own sounds with their wings, and bats squeak. If you listen carefully you can hear the bats when they fly by at dusk in search of mosquitoes and other insects.

New flowers continue to open, offering many new fragrances. Berries and other summer fruits ripen, adding to the delicate summer smells. Berries, mints, and a variety of fruits will be yours to taste.

A pleasant way to allow all your senses to enjoy the summer is to find a safe place to lie down and be very still. Concentrate on looking, feeling, smelling, and listening. You can also imagine tasting. Shut your eyes. Think of eating a strawberry or raspberry. Can you taste it? Summer is a rich and pleasant season. Enjoy it with all your senses.

Spittlebugs

Wherever you find clover, grass, and other green plants is a good place to search for spittlebugs. Look for a glob of white froth on a green stem. Here is where you stop to hunt for the "spitter."

The froth is not really spit. It is a harmless substance made by the spittlebug, an insect in its nymph, or immature, stage. Eventually, the nymph will develop into an adult insect known as a froghopper. As a nymph, the spittlebug must have a moist and cool environment.

It provides just the right atmosphere for itself by manufacturing a glob of froth. At first you might not readily find the insect, but keep looking. Pick up a mass of froth. It feels like beaten egg white. The nymph is green, like the stem on which it is feeding. It has two little dark eyes and hangs upside down.

While the downward part of the insect sucks the plant juices, the other end pours out the spitlike substance which it mixes with air to produce the protective froth.

You may safely remove the nymph from its stalk, and carefully place it on a fresh stem. After five minutes or so, the spittlebug will face head down and begin feeding. Watch it as it produces a new spittle cover for itself. Few things are more fascinating.

Toward the end of summer, the spittlebug stops feeding and changes into an adult. The adult is a small, brown insect that resembles a tiny frog, as it jumps from plant to plant. Now it is called a froghopper.

After mating, the female froghopper lays her eggs in a plant stem where they rest all winter. The adult froghoppers die, but the eggs will hatch next spring and provide a new crop of spittlebugs to decorate the plants with their "spit" once again.

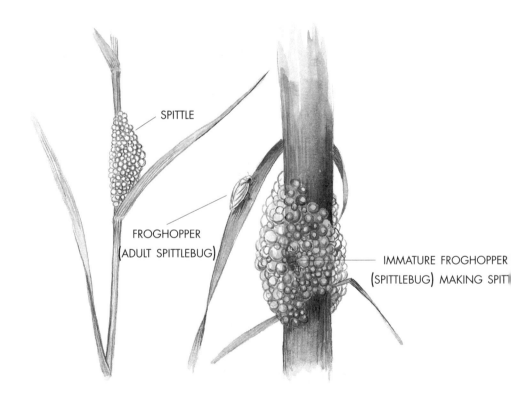

SPITTLE

FROGHOPPER
(ADULT SPITTLEBUG)

IMMATURE FROGHOPPER
(SPITTLEBUG) MAKING SPIT

White Man's Foot

Walk across a yard, lawn, vacant lot, crack in the pavement, or along a road. You are certain to have stepped on a white man's foot. White man's foot is a plant that seems able to grow anywhere. Take a nearby safari to find and examine this interesting flowering plant. Why is it found everywhere? What makes it so successful?

This plant is usually called plantain or common plantain. The American Indians gave it the name white man's foot. Originally, the seeds came to this country from Europe. There were probably seeds in packing materials, as well as on the hoofs of cattle and on people's feet. When the seeds landed on American soil, they took root and flourished. Conditions here favored these foreign plants.

The Indians knew that plantain was not native, and they soon associated the plant with the white settlers. They decided that the white man had been wherever they saw plantain, so they called the plant white man's foot.

Henry Wadsworth Longfellow used the Indians' name for plantain in his famous poem *Song of Hiawatha.*

> *Whereso'er they tread, beneath them*
> *Springs a flower unknown among us,*
> *Springs the White-man's Foot in blossom.*

To find white man's foot, look for a circle of flat leaves that hug the ground. You can imagine the leaves resemble a circle of flat tongues. A spike about 18 inches (45 centimeters) tall grows straight up from the center, looking somewhat like a rat's tail. All along the stalk grow tiny, greenish white flowers, which will form many sticky, little seeds. The seeds catch onto the feet of people and animals and are carried about until they fall off. They can grow and thrive in any kind of soil, and this is how the plant spreads.

Remove one of the leaves. Notice that there are several ribs on each leaf. All of the ribs run from the stem of the leaf to the edge of the leaf. The largest rib is in the center. Three or four more are on either side of it. The leaf's food and water are transported up and down in canals inside these ribs. The ribs are made of strong cells. The rest of the leaf is soft.

It is said that the American Indians used the strong ribs in surgery. The ribs were removed from the leaves and used as surgical thread to sew skin together after an operation.

Pick a leaf and gently remove the soft tissue between the ribs. Try not to break the ribs. After all the soft tissue has been removed, the remaining part of the leaf resembles a stringed instrument somewhat like a banjo.

Fireflies–Nature's Magic Lanterns

Many animals are active at night. Among these are insects we call fireflies, glowworms, or lightening bugs. One of the summer's great pleasures is to watch these tiny, living lanterns flash on and off. Plan a safari to a place where you can observe them.

A patch of lawn in a backyard or a nearby meadow makes a perfect stage. The best time of day is just after the sun sets. The flashing lights continue throughout the early evening.

Fireflies are not flies, worms, or bugs. They belong to the large group of insects known as beetles. Beetles have two pairs of wings. A top, stiff pair of wings covers and protects two delicate flight wings beneath it.

Fireflies are small, oblong beetles. They are about 0.75 inch (2 centimeters) long. These dull-colored, brownish beetles can be found crawling among damp leaves on the ground during the day. However, as the day ends, the males fly up in the air to flash their mating signals. This is when the sparkling light show begins.

The insects flash their lights on as they fly up and turn them off as they come down. There are many different kinds of fireflies, and each has a certain set of signals. The females wait

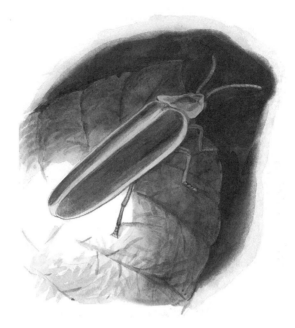

below on grasses, bushes, or the ground. When a female recognizes the right signal from a male of her own kind, she responds with a special blink. The male then flies down to her and they mate.

After mating, the female lays her eggs in the soil or among fallen leaves on the ground. Some eggs glow and look like shining dots at night. In about four weeks, the eggs hatch into wormlike larvae. The larvae of some fireflies glow. This is how the name *glowworm* originated. The larvae live underground for at least a year before changing into adult fireflies. Some spend two years underground.

The adult stage of a firefly is a short one. Adults do not feed at all. They spend all their time finding mates, mating, and laying eggs. When this is done, they die.

Live adults are easy to catch and examine. When you find one, turn it over. The lower part of the body is yellow. This is the part that lights up. The glowing section is larger in males than in females.

The light of the firefly is produced by two chemicals inside the insect's body. It is a cold light, which is different from the light produced by an electric bulb. An electric bulb heats up because most of its energy is given off as heat. All of the energy made by the chemicals in the firefly is turned into light. You can actually read by the light of fireflies if you collect enough of them in a small jar. Be sure to set the insects free when you are through observing them.

If you should care to flirt with a firefly, you need a flashlight, a ticking watch, and patience. Sit or lie on the ground. Study the lighting pattern of a firefly. These are the things to observe: How long does the flash last? How many times does it blink each time it starts its flash? How much time passes between each set of signals? How much time does it take for the female to respond?

As you watch fireflies blink on and off, think of them as living stars–tiny shooting stars visiting the earth.

Plants–Outdoor Air Conditioners

People use air conditioners to make the indoors more comfortable in hot, humid weather. These appliances are made to improve the air inside a room by filtering out air impurities and regulating the temperature.

Green plants do the same thing outdoors by filtering out the particles that pollute the air. Plants also cool the air. In addition, green plants remove carbon dioxide from the outdoor environment.

Carbon dioxide is a gas that comes from industrial manufacturing processes, from all kinds of burning, and from automobile exhausts. There is also carbon dioxide in the breath, which people and all other living things give off.

Using energy from the sun, green leaves make food from carbon dioxide and water. While they are manufacturing food, they give off oxygen. Oxygen freshens the air. It is an essential gas for all living things.

The trees in a park can remove about half of the air pollution that collects there. It has also been estimated that one tree has the cooling effect of five air conditioners.

Find out how plants air-condition the outdoors. Place a thermometer on a grassy spot on the ground next to a paved area, such as a driveway. After a few minutes, read the thermometer and make a record of your reading. Now place the thermometer on the paved part of the driveway. Leave it in place for the same length of time as before and then take your second reading. Compare the temperature of the soil with that of the pavement. Which is cooler?

Using your thermometer, compare the air in a group of trees with the air where the ground is bare. Hold the thermometer at the height of your nose. You can also compare the air temperature along a road with the air temperature along a trail. You can probably think of other places to make comparisons of air temperatures. You will be surprised to find out how much plants cool the air on a hot summer day.

People have always enjoyed plants for their beauty. Now you know how plants can also refresh and improve our environment. This is true all over the world. Our planet needs even more plants. Perhaps you can plant some and get your friends to do the same. We should also prevent the destruction of plants that are now growing, wherever they are.

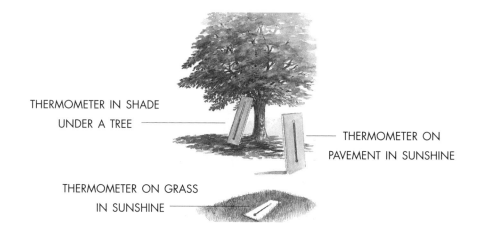

THERMOMETER IN SHADE
UNDER A TREE

THERMOMETER ON
PAVEMENT IN SUNSHINE

THERMOMETER ON GRASS
IN SUNSHINE

Shooting Stars

Bits of matter from outer space are constantly falling to earth. As they speed downward, they rub against other particles. This friction causes the bits of matter to light up like stars in flight. Although we call them shooting stars or falling stars, they are not stars at all. They are particles of dust from planets in outer space. Properly known as meteors, most of them burn up quickly in the atmosphere.

When a meteor strikes the earth, it is called a meteorite. Meteorites are made of stone or metal. This planetary metal may be iron or nickel. A meteorite may be as small as a grain of sand or as large as a giant boulder. Large meteorites can make great big holes in the ground, called craters, although this seldom happens.

Millions of the tiny meteorites keep falling on the earth's surface. They form a kind of planetary dust. You can try to collect some of this dust. All you need is a magnet. Pull the magnet through a bare patch of topsoil and look at the small particles clinging to it. Some of these particles may be planetary dust–iron and nickel from outer space.

You may see meteors on most summer nights. However, for a really exciting night show, plan a safari to watch for meteors after midnight on August 12. This is the date that, each year, meteors fall in large numbers. Instead of seeing one or two meteors, you may witness a shower of visitors from outer space.

A Primrose Surprise

Long twilights at this time of year provide opportunities for unusual summer safaris. Twilight is a magical time of day. Even after the sun has set, the sky retains a bright glow for some time before darkness comes on. This is the perfect time to solve the mystery concerning the closed buds of the evening primrose.

The evening primrose is a common plant, which grows in dry soil. You may find it along roadsides, in fence corners, and right in your own backyard. The plant consists of a plain brown stalk that grows from 1 to 6 feet (30 to 180 centimeters) tall. By day it has both faded yellow flowers and closed buds bunched together on top. The drooping blossoms give off a faint whisper of fragrance.

However, if you take your walk at sundown, the same brown stalk becomes an entirely different plant. As the sun sets, the buds begin to expand. They open up to become beautiful flowers with four glowing petals and a powerful lemon scent. The flowers may be anywhere from 1 to 2 inches (2.5 to 5 centimeters) across. The petals form a long tube. Nectar is produced at the bottom of this tube.

Only those insects whose tongues are at least 1 inch (2.5 centimeters) long can reach into this pool of nectar. At night the nectar is food for several kinds of moths. The moths, flying about at night, are attracted to the evening primrose by its strong fragrance.

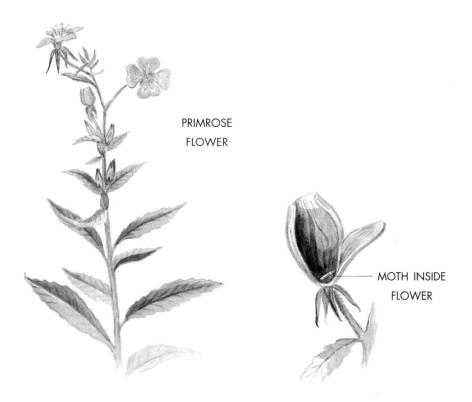

PRIMROSE
FLOWER

MOTH INSIDE
FLOWER

There is a little, pink and yellow moth that often visits these flowers. If you examine the plant in the daytime, you might find one of these moths tucked in a blossom, asleep. Only the yellow of its wings shows. Birds searching for insects would pass it by because the moth looks like part of the faded petals. The old flowers fall off during the day. Each flower leaves behind a capsule with new evening primrose seeds developing inside.

Only a few buds open each night–sometimes only one flower appears. However, the plant has a long season. You can find the flowers blooming all summer and into October. If an open flower has no visitor during the night, it may remain open for a few hours in the morning. At such times, a bumblebee or a hummingbird may pause for a sip of nectar. As summer ends, the evening primrose may remain open all day.

Now, what about the mystery of the closed buds? You can only solve this in the daytime. Examine the closed buds of several evening primrose stalks. There are two kinds of closed buds: Long, thin buds and short, fat ones. The long ones will open in the evening to form the fragrant, yellow flowers. The short ones will never open into flowers.

To find out why, examine the short buds. Some of them have little holes. Some of them are without holes. Open one without a hole. Tear it or cut it open very carefully. You will find a small, whitish caterpillar inside. In a few weeks, the caterpillar will change into a very small moth. Before it is completely transformed, the insect makes a little escape hole. The caterpillar has been feeding on the insides of the flower. The injured flower is, therefore, unable to open. Now you have solved the mystery of the closed buds. Nature is full of surprises.

A Gem on Wings

Midsummer is the best time to seek a gold fortune. You can find one such treasure in the form of a golden beetle. It feeds on the leaves of the wild morning glory, a common plant that is also called hedge bindweed and lady's nightcap. The wild morning glory grows as a vine, climbing over fences, stone walls, and other plants. It grows in vacant city lots as well as in the country.

The wild morning glory opens fully at the beginning of the day and closes at sunset. The bell-shaped flower is large–about 2 inches (5 centimeters) long. It is all white or pink with white stripes. The name *lady's nightcap* comes from the shape and color of the blossom.

Examine the undersides of the flower's arrow-shaped leaves. This is the place to look for the gold. The golden beetle makes large holes in the leaf as it feeds. Hold a small, open bottle in one hand while you search for your treasure. As soon as you spot your gem, shake it into the bottle.

In a few seconds, you will see several marvelous transformations. Each time the beetle changes, it resembles a different jewel. On the leaf it looks like a piece of molten gold. Once it is

GOLDEN BEETLE

in the bottle, the gold disappears and becomes a bright opal. Then it changes to a milky white jewel of mother-of-pearl. Sometimes it resembles a bit of coral. Finally the insect turns dull orange. Keep looking. It often changes to gold once more.

The beetles feed actively all summer. When the weather turns cold, they hide under the bark of a tree or among the leaves on the ground. They remain hidden and protected from the cold until the following spring. They often live for two years. The adults mate, then the females lay eggs on the morning glory leaves. The eggs hatch into caterpillars. Like other insects, the caterpillars feed and grow, passing through several stages. Finally they turn into adult golden beetles.

You can plan a different and exciting summer safari. Find where the wild morning glory grows and search for a bit of living gold.

Watching Summer Clouds

The sun makes the seasons. The sun also explains the reasons for different kinds of weather. Consider the clouds. Clouds form in the atmosphere from water vapor that rises from the earth.

If you leave a dish of water uncovered, the water will gradually disappear. The liquid water changes into water vapor, an invisible gas. The gas slowly rises into the air. When it reaches the cold of the upper air, the vapor turns back into water. Cold air cannot hold as much vapor as warm air. You can see this when you place a glass of ice water on a table. Drops of water appear on the outside of the glass. The water drops come from the water vapor of the cooled air around the glass. The water vapor condenses, or changes, into a liquid.

Water evaporates from all sources of water on earth–puddles, ponds, lakes, rivers, and oceans–especially when summer days are long and hot. Water vapor is also given off by the leaves of plants. The breath and sweat from people and other animals also contain water vapor.

All this water vapor rises in the atmosphere, where the lower temperature causes the vapor to condense into drops of water. If

the temperature in the upper atmosphere is very cold, the vapor forms ice crystals. The condensed water particles attach themselves to bits of dust or smoke, and clouds are formed. There are several different kinds of clouds.

The most interesting summer clouds are the large, puffy ones known as cumulus clouds. They resemble heaps of fluffy white cotton. Cumulus clouds form when heated air from the earth rises straight up. Look for these cotton-candy-like clouds on bright, sunny days. They usually appear in the late morning or early afternoon. They disappear toward evening. People call them fair-weather clouds. Plan to spend time watching them on a lovely summer afternoon.

Spread a blanket in your backyard and enjoy some cloud watching. You will discover some new things about clouds. They are forever changing their shapes. What pictures can you see? Do they tell a story? Observe that not all the clouds are moving in the same direction. Can you find rows of clouds on different levels moving in different directions at the same time? Or clouds breaking away from other clouds? Notice that some clouds join together and become larger clouds. Try to compose a poem about clouds.

This safari may be one of the shortest but most imaginative adventures.

The Red Eft and the Newt

Did you ever come across a little, orange-red animal on the ground that resembled a miniature dinosaur? It was probably no bigger than your middle finger and was very colorful. Did you look closely enough to see a line of bright red dots on its orange coat along both sides of its body? Was each dot surrounded by a frame of black specks? You have seen a red eft. Red efts are salamanders and are related to frogs. They can be seen in the woods or along a wet part of a road.

Plan to go on safari to a place where you may find red efts. A damp, shady corner in your backyard is a likely spot. Another promising place is along a road after a rain when the ground is still moist.

When you find one, you may pick it up carefully and safely hold it in your hand. This animal has a very interesting life history. It spends part of its life on land and part in the water. This orange stage is the land form.

The eft lives among damp mosses and leaves, and it feeds on very tiny animals. It remains on land for about three years. Then, in the spring of that final year, it feels an urge to return to the water. It searches for a pond or shallow stream where water plants grow. When it reaches the water it changes into a newt.

Its skin loses its orange color and turns olive-green on top and tan below. The red and black spots remain. Male newts have large hind legs. The females are somewhat lighter in color than the males. They are also smaller, and have more delicate legs. Newts live in the water for the rest of their lives. A newt lives for about seven years.

Male and female newts mate in the water. The mother newt then lays her fertilized eggs, one at a time, on the leaves of a water plant. She deposits about a hundred eggs. After a few weeks, the eggs hatch. At first, each little eft looks and acts very much like a fish. Several weeks pass, and another change takes place. The efts develop legs, begin to look less like fish, and finally crawl out on land. Their coats are now changed to an orange-red. It is during their few years on land that you will find the beautiful little animals on your walks.

You may go on safari to ponds and streams where you can search for the adult newts, and you may take walks on land where you can find the red efts. These are two stages of a very interesting animal.

NEWT (ADULT)

RED EFT
(IMMATURE)

Monarch Butterflies

Summer is filled with many different colors. Birds and flowers contribute to the colorful landscape. So do insects. Among the brightest insects are the monarch butterflies.

Monarch butterflies are large. Their wingspan is about 4 inches (10 centimeters) wide. You see only a few of them at the beginning of the season. Toward the end of summer, more and more of these orange and black butterflies fill the air. The best place for you to find them is where the common milkweed grows. The life of the monarch butterfly depends on this plant. Plan some summer safaris to a patch of milkweed.

Milkweed is found almost everywhere where the soil is dry: Along roadsides, in fields, and in backyards. They are tall plants, growing 3 feet or more (about 1 meter) high. Their large, oblong leaves grow opposite each other. If you bruise the leaves or the stem, a thick, white, milky juice oozes out. This liquid may be poisonous to some birds and other insects, but not to the monarchs. Clusters of lavender-brown flowers grow where the leaves are joined to the stalk. The blossoms are very fragrant and produce an abundance of nectar. The nectar is free of the poison that is found in the rest of the plant.

Examine the undersides of the milkweed leaves, especially those near the top. Look for something that resembles a small, pale green jewel. This is the egg of the monarch butterfly. Make a series of forays to where you find the egg and be prepared to witness one of nature's great miracles: The development of this tiny egg into an adult butterfly.

In about five days, the egg hatches into a little caterpillar with yellow, black, and white stripes. The caterpillar devours many milkweed leaves and grows rapidly. When its skin becomes too tight, the larva sheds it and grows a new one. This happens four times. Between each shed, or molt, the caterpillar increases in size.

In about two weeks, after the fourth molt, the caterpillar is about 2 inches (5 centimeters) long. It stops eating and finds a resting place. It selects a branch, a twig, or the underside of a fence rail. There it spins a pad of silk. Then it attaches itself to the pad, hanging upside down. Its shape now resembles the letter *J.*

After a few hours, it changes its shape as it twists and thrashes about. The larva grows short and thick as it quiets down. It encloses itself in a pale green covering decorated with shining flecks of gold across its surface. It looks like a living jewel. This is the third, or pupal, stage when the insect is called a chrysalis.

Ten or twelve days later, the adult butterfly appears. When its green covering turns transparent, and you can see the orange and black butterfly folded up inside, get ready for a dramatic performance.

A weak, crumpled butterfly emerges from its chrysalis and hangs on to the colorless shell. Its wings stiffen as liquid from the insect's body is pumped into them. Soon the butterfly becomes strong and beautiful. It begins to fly about, sipping nectar from wildflowers as it prepares to go forth. Where will it go?

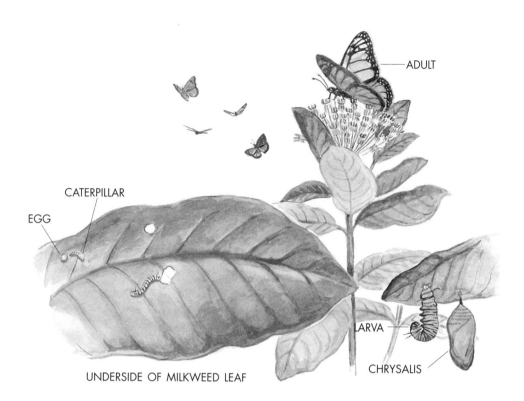

ADULT

CATERPILLAR

EGG

LARVA

CHRYSALIS

UNDERSIDE OF MILKWEED LEAF

If autumn is near, it will migrate south, joining millions of other monarchs. They will all fly to some very cool, moist mountains in central Mexico, where they will gather in huge masses on trees and vines. The clusters of butterflies hang there motionless throughout the winter. A ray of sunshine during the day may provide enough energy for some of them to flutter their wings a bit.

At the first signs of spring there is a burst of mating activity as males rush about seeking females. The males die after mating, and the females start flying north, laying their eggs on fresh milkweed plants along the way. The females die after all their eggs are laid, and their offspring continue the return flight. It takes several generations of monarchs to complete the trip home.

The monarch butterfly that you see in the summer is not the same one that departed last fall. It may belong to the third or fourth generation. Very few of the original travelers that fly south in autumn survive a return trip. The fall migrants are the only monarchs that are strong enough to make the long trip all the way to Mexico.

Watch for monarch butterflies that fly south at the end of summer. They may be on their way to Mexico.

Cheerful Chirping Sparrows

Are English sparrows cheerful? No one really knows. But when you listen to them, they certainly sound chipper. These sparrows are small, brown, streaked birds that almost always appear in groups. The groups are usually made up of birds of different sexes and ages. They generally travel in families or in large communities. They forever chirp and cheep as if in constant communication with one another.

These birds were brought to this country from England in 1852. They nest four or five times a year, laying about five eggs each time. As a result, the English sparrow population increased rapidly. The birds are now found all over the United States. Wherever there are people, there are buildings. Wherever there are buildings, you are sure to find some resident sparrows.

The English sparrow is also called the house sparrow. It often nests in a cavity, perhaps in a building where there is a loose clapboard, a space left by a missing brick, a clogged drainspout, or a bird box. The nesting material consists of some grass, feathers, and assorted trash. Sometimes it nests in a tree or shrub, weaving a dome-shaped nest with a side entrance out of all sorts of stuff, such as string, paper, bits of rags, and straw.

The English sparrow provides an opportunity to observe the family behavior of birds. First, find a group of sparrows. Then make frequent visits to that spot. The chances are that your own backyard will be the best place. All you have to do is go out and watch them. They will probably arrive at about the same time each day.

Get acquainted with the individuals in your group. The handsome male is bright brown above and whitish gray below. His throat has a black bib, and his cheeks are white. The female is a duller brown, lacks the bib, and has a pale stripe over each eye. The young resemble the females, but their feathers are browner on top and their beaks, legs, and feet are pinkish.

There are many interesting things to learn about the behavior of English sparrows. Listen to the sounds they make. Males make special sounds when they communicate with females. You can follow their conversation even if the birds are some distance apart. Listen for different sounds. Perhaps you can figure out what they mean. For example, the birds chirp in a certain way before a rain. Listen for another kind of chirping when they gather in very large flocks at dusk.

What chirps do the young make as they follow their parents and beg for food? Find a baby who is not following its parents. It may sit hunched up, chirping differently. An adult sparrow passing by will probably pop something into its mouth.

Sparrows usually peck on the ground for food. What foods do they choose? You might scatter a handful of different foods on one of your trips. Which do they seem to prefer?

How do they fly? These birds prefer low bushes. They spread their wings out in flight, then fold them in as they enter among the leaves.

What other behaviors can you observe? For example, are they peaceful or aggressive? Is there a pecking order when they feed? Do they hop or walk on the ground? After a while you will recognize individuals and really enjoy observing the life of the English sparrow. You may even feel like part of the family.

Katydids–Insect Fiddlers

Katydids are beautiful, large insects, about 2 inches (5 centimeters) long. They have broad, bright green outer wing covers that resemble leaves. The covers protect their strong flying wings underneath. The flying wings remain folded like a fan when not in use.

Sometime in August, toward the end of the day, the katydids begin to call. Night after night, more of them join the chorus. You may hear a loud "Katy did," a shorter "She didn't," or a mild "Katy." It sounds as if they are all having an ongoing argument. The calls of the katydids are longer and more vigorous on warm summer nights. As the temperature drops, their sounds become softer and shorter.

Like other insects, the katydid does not have a true voice. The wings of the male produce the rasping sound. The male scrapes a file on his left wing across a rough surface on his right wing.

The chorus, which can become very loud at times, is a song of courtship. The males sing to attract the females. When a female katydid hears a male sing, she is listening, not with her heart, but with her legs. Katydids have ears located on the upper part of their front legs.

After a pair of katydids mate, the female pastes her fertilized eggs onto twigs and branches. Young katydids will hatch the following spring. At first they will look like small, incomplete adults. They will molt and grow until they mature into complete adults and are ready to join the chorus.

Katydids are hard to find, although if you hunt for them, you can succeed. You will probably find them in a tree or a bush, chewing on green leaves. Notice the position of their long antennae. One points forward and one back.

How good a hunter are you? Plan a safari to find out. Go outdoors toward the end of the day. Even if you do not see katydids, you will surely hear them. When you discover one or more, remember the date. Some people say that six weeks after the first katydid calls, you can expect the first frost.

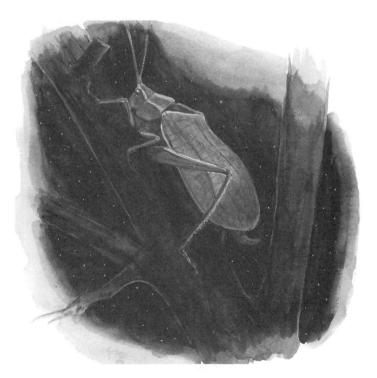

Charming Chipmunks

Everyone loves chipmunks. Have you ever seen two chipmunks approach each other and pause to rub noses as if they were kissing? They have many gestures that will surely win your heart. Chipmunks are friendly, energetic, and easily trained.

These appealing little creatures are about 10 inches (25 centimeters) long. They have brown fur with five dark stripes on their backs. When you gaze into their big eyes, it is hard to believe that chipmunks are related to rats and mice.

As summer winds down, chipmunks get busy storing food for a long, cold winter. Watch them stuff their cheeks full of food, disappear somewhere, and come right back to gather more. Their cheeks can stretch into large pouches. Now and then, you may see them sitting on a fence or a rock as they call, "Chip-chip-chip." Perhaps they are resting.

Chipmunks save a great deal of food in special storerooms in their long, underground burrows. Chipmunks take long naps in their burrows in cold weather. They sleep in cozy bedrooms on mattresses made of leaves. Besides using storerooms, they also put some food under their beds. This makes it easy for them to nibble on a snack now and then.

The outside entrance to a chipmunk's burrow is hidden. It could be under some rocks, logs, or plant roots. Sometimes a chipmunk will dig its den under a building.

Finding chipmunks is easy. They will be dashing here and there in your backyard or garden. Plan to take a camera on your chipmunk hunt. You are sure to get some interesting snapshots. Pictures are wonderful trophies to bring home from a safari.

What are the chipmunks eating? It would be interesting for you to scatter a variety of foods on the ground. Do they prefer certain foods? How often do they feed? Try to get a picture of one feeding. Chipmunks become very friendly when they are fed. Don't be surprised if these wild pets return next year for more of the peanuts they enjoyed this summer.

CHIPMUNK IN WINTER BURROW

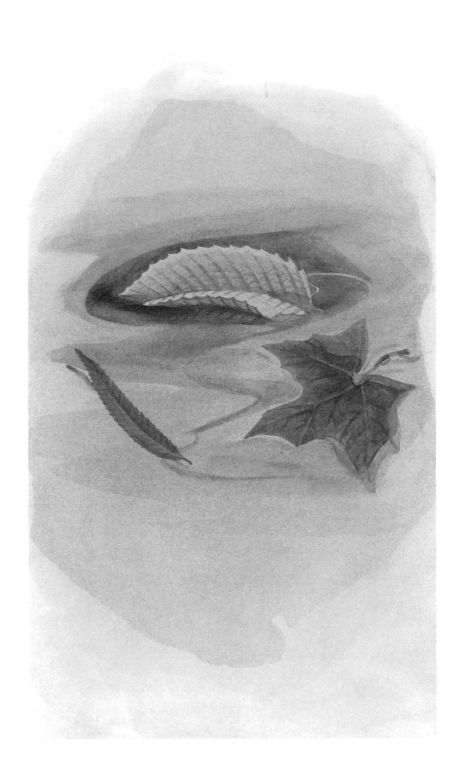

AUTUMN

Autumn is a glorious season. The hot, humid summer gradually gives way to brisk, cool days. Autumn arrives on September 22 or 23. It ends thirteen weeks later. On the day when autumn officially arrives, there are twelve daylight hours and twelve nighttime hours.

From then on, the days get shorter and shorter. The nights grow longer and longer. Shorter days mean fewer hours of sunlight and cooler weather ahead.

Many changes take place in autumn. The last of the wildflowers bloom. Seeds that will produce next year's plants travel around. Leaves change color and many fall to the ground. Fruits ripen. Plants and animals prepare for winter. There are also sky and weather changes.

Autumn is an invigorating time. It feels good to get outdoors, and it is a wonderful time to plan safaris. In autumn, you can see the many changes taking place in our world.

Falling Leaves

In autumn the leaves of many trees change their colors and quietly fall to the ground. This is probably why *fall* is another name for *autumn.* Some trees, such as pines, are green all year. Because of this, they are called evergreen. They usually have narrow, needlelike leaves. Evergreens also shed their leaves, but not all at once.

Before leaves fall, they lose their green color. They turn yellow, brown, and red, as well as a variety of mixed colors, according to the kind of trees from which they fell. The change makes the landscape look like a beautiful tapestry.

While a green leaf is on a tree, it manufactures food for the tree. Before it falls, most of the nourishment that remains in the leaf travels into the tree trunk and roots where it will be stored all winter. This stored food will provide nourishment for next year's spring leaves and flowers. Fallen leaves mix with the soil, making it richer.

It is fun to find a pile of dry, fallen leaves and walk through it. Listen to the pleasant, swooshing sounds you make.

Look at the leaves lying on the ground. Some are upside down

and some are right side up. Collect one hundred fallen leaves in the position that they have fallen. How many fell right side up? How many fell upside down?

What are the colors of the fallen leaves? Are there more leaves of one color than another? What is that color? If you recognize one kind of tree–such as an oak, apple, or maple–see how many colors you can find on that one tree.

Find a small pile of leaves. Brush aside the top ones, which are probably this year's leaves. Find the layer of last year's leaves. How are they different from those that fell this year? Can you find some leaves that you think may have fallen two years ago? What happens to fallen leaves as they get older? Gently move the leaves aside until you get down to the soil. Notice how dark and crumbly old leaves become. Finally they become part of the soil. Old, decayed leaves nourish the soil and improve its texture.

In the spring and summer, the green leaves used the energy from the sun to manufacture food. Energy from the food was passed on to all parts of the tree. In the autumn, the remaining energy in the fallen leaves passes to the soil. Here it provides strength for new life to develop the following year. This is a cycle of energy.

The energy cycle is one wonderful example of how our world works.

Yellow Jackets Love Picnics

It's easy to recognize the wasps that we call yellow jackets by the bands of yellow and black around their bodies. Only the queen yellow jackets survive the winter. Early in May, a queen begins to build her community nest. She lays a few eggs and feeds the young. When these young workers mature, they take over the job of enlarging the nest and caring for the many more developing yellow jackets. From then on, all the queen does is lay more and more eggs. As fall approaches, there may be thousands of wasps in the nest of each queen. By September and October, yellow jackets seem to be everywhere, especially where there is food.

Some yellow jackets build their thin, round, papery nest in the ground. Others choose trees or the sides of buildings. The German, or "picnic," yellow jacket chooses the inside of an old house as its preferred location.

Young yellow jackets eat insects and spiders. They need a meat diet to develop properly. The adults eat anything and everything. The picnic wasp is sure to attend any outdoor event where food is served. They have learned to eat the same kinds of food that people eat. It is not unusual to find one sharing your sandwich, whether it is ham, tuna fish, or peanut butter and jelly.

Plan some fall safaris to places where food is available. You will be sure to find yellow jackets there and learn something interesting about their food habits. You might look in a fruit orchard or even in a backyard where there is a single fruit tree. A roadside stand would be another good choice. You will also find yellow jackets hovering over bits of food in discarded trash along the roadside or wherever ripened fruits have fallen on the ground. The wasps also sip nectar from flowers.

If you are stung by a yellow jacket, be prepared to flee. These insects make repeated stings. Do not kill the insect that stung you. Squashing it will release the poison into the air. The chemicals in the poison will stimulate other yellow jackets to attack you.

Pain from a sting could last for hours. Apply some ice to the place where you were stung. Ice reduces the pain and swelling, and also prevents the poison from spreading through your body.

UNDERGROUND NEST

Some people are highly sensitive to the poison released by bees, yellow jackets, and other stinging insects. They start to sneeze and find it hard to breathe after being stung. Should you suffer such a reaction, get to a doctor at once. If you know that you are sensitive to stinging insects, it would be best to avoid this safari.

When on safari, follow a few precautions to keep from getting stung. Wear light-colored clothes. Dark clothing seems to make the yellow jackets more aggressive. Do not use any perfume or fragrant shampoo, soap, etc. Yellow jackets are attracted to floral scents. Move slowly and do not make any sudden gestures. The wasps are programmed to defend their families and will sting only when they feel threatened. Do not eat while you are observing them.

If you see one of the insects on a piece of meat, observe how it carves out a small section and then flies off with it. This is probably intended to feed the young back at the nest. What kinds of food do yellow jackets eat? Do they seem to show a preference for certain foods?

If you see some yellow jackets come out of the ground, there may be a nest underground. The entrance is about as large as a mouse hole. Follow the direction in which some yellow jackets fly after feeding. You might spy one flying to its nest in a tree or some other likely place in the area. There are many other interesting things to find out about yellow jackets as you continue to watch them.

When the weather turns cold, all members of the wasp colony die. Only the queen survives. She will seek shelter for the winter under a stone, among moss, under leaves, or in a crack of the thick bark of a tree. There she will remain until the following spring when she emerges to start a new colony.

A Flower's Hidden Marriage

Violets are early spring flowers that come in many colors, but the most common ones are purple. After the spring blossoms are gone, seedpods develop. When the seeds are ripe, the pods open, scattering their seeds. These will produce new violets the following spring. Although the flowers are gone, the violet leaves continue to grow and make food for the plant and also for some hidden flowers growing at its base.

These hidden flowers are a mystery. In order to find them, plan a fall safari to a place where violets grow. Although violets bloom in shady spots, they are also found in many sunny locations. A piece of lawn or a patch of grass in a backyard is suitable for violets.

Find a bunch of violet leaves in early fall. Brush aside some soil at the base of the plant and any dead leaves that may have collected there. Find the pale green buds on the short stalks. These are the mysterious violet flowers that remain hidden all summer as they develop.

These flowers never open. They lack the bright colors of spring violets. However, even though they remain closed, the flowers produce seeds. Pick one of these flowers and open it. You will find a pod of unripe, pearly white seeds. Plan another trip in October or November. Now the developed pods have split open into three equal parts, each filled with black, ripened seeds. These seeds will give rise to many more spring flowers.

The violet's way of producing concealed seeds is called a hidden marriage, because the flower never opens. The processes of pollination and fertilization remain hidden in the closed bud.

Woodchucks Prepare for Winter

Woodchucks spend about half their lives in underground burrows. This is probably why they are also called groundhogs. These animals are easy to find. Look for a woodchuck den where a backyard is near a field or the woods. Woodchucks are plant eaters and spend all summer eating, sleeping, and avoiding enemies.

Autumn finds the groundhog eating more and sleeping less. It does take time out to dig its winter den, a protected burrow for its long, cold weather nap. It selects a place near woody plants. When the snow falls, the fluffy ice crystals collect among the plant stems, forming a warm, winter blanket.

Even though the animal is busy with its chores, it is very alert. If it hears you or any other sound, it pops straight up and sniffs the air for a possible enemy. This is when you can get a good look at the woodchuck. You may even have time to take its picture if you wish.

A woodchuck's burrow has several entrances. The main entrance is built beneath a rock or a tree stump, and slopes down for a ways. The others are not so easy to detect. The woodchuck seldom wanders far from one of the entrances. If it senses danger, it can make a quick retreat through one of the holes to the safety of its den.

The woodchuck grows so fat during autumn that it can hardly walk. Much of what it has eaten has turned into fat, which will nourish the woodchuck all winter. One fall day, the woodchuck suddenly stops feeding, even though plenty of food is still available.

A message from its brain has sent a signal that it is time to start its winter sleep.

This long sleep, called hibernation, will last until spring. The woodchuck empties its bowels and its bladder outside several times before entering the den. Then it plugs up the entrance from inside the den by pushing soil against the hole. It rolls up into a ball and remains down in the burrow as if frozen for about six months.

Although February 2 is Groundhog Day, all groundhogs do not leave their burrows on that date. Some time in February or March, only the males will leave their burrows to search for female partners. After visiting a female in her burrow and mating, each male returns to his den, and all wait for spring.

While on safari, find out when woodchucks feed and what foods they choose. Try to find the sloping entrance hole to the den. Watch the creature pop into its hole when you move.

HIBERNATING
WOODCHUCK

Sumac–a Treat for Birds and People

Sumac, considered to be a small tree or shrub, announces early in the season that autumn is on its way. Its clear yellow or fiery red leaves and bright red fruits signal the beginning of the fall parade of colors. Early in the fall, the plant provides a feast for the eyes. Throughout the year, it provides a tasty drink.

Sumac is abundant and easily found. Look for it along roadsides and in vacant lots where soils are dry and poor. It may grow singly or in bunches. A group of sumacs is called a thicket.

There are several kinds of sumacs, but the two most common ones are the smooth sumac and the staghorn sumac. The staghorn sumac has fuzzy hairs on its twigs and branches. Look at this plant in the fall after the leaves have dropped. The upper branches are spread apart and resemble a stag's horns. It looks particularly attractive when seen against the sun.

Both varieties of sumac have bunches of wine-colored fruits that last all winter. Either one can be used to make a drink that is delicious and rich in vitamin C. There is a variety called poison sumac. It grows in wet places and its fruits are white. Never use white berries. The red ones are perfectly safe. Indians collected the red sumac fruits and used them throughout the year.

To prepare a sumac drink, collect the fruit from either the smooth or the staghorn sumac, or from a mixture of both. Pull several bunches of fruits from the plants and place them in a large pot. Cover with cold water. You may let this steep until the water turns a deep pink, or you may heat it slowly until the desired color appears. Do not boil it. Strain the mixture through cheesecloth and sweeten the beverage with honey as the Indians did. You may also use sugar. The drink, called sumacade by some, is delicious either hot or cold.

This is one safari in which you can become acquainted with an easily available wild food. Birds and other wildlife do not seem to prefer sumac fruits. However, the berries do provide them with a source of nourishment during severe storms or when food becomes scarce in winter. You may even find some birds feeding in a sumac while you are gathering fall fruits for your own use.

SUMAC PLANT

SUMACADE

HONEY

Fuzzy Little Woolly Bears

Have you ever thought of going on safari to hunt for bears? You can do it right in your own backyard or along a road. The bears you will be hunting are those that crawl about in the fall. They are little fuzzy caterpillars called woolly bears. They are red-brown at the center and black at each end.

The march of the woolly bears starts sometime in September. A favorite place for them is on a piece of paved road in the sunlight. It may be the warmth of the sun that attracts them. Most caterpillars creep along rather slowly, but woolly bears seem to be in a hurry. They are hungry and in search of food.

This little animal hatched in the spring from an insect egg laid by a yellow moth, the Isabella Tiger moth. Since then, the woolly bear, which is the larval stage of the moth, has spent most of its time feeding. It feasts on many kinds of green leaves, especially dandelion greens.

Gradually, as the temperature drops, its feasting slows down. When the time comes for the woolly bear to go into winter hibernation, it stops feeding altogether. It finds a protective spot, rolls up into a little ball, and waits until springtime. You may find it

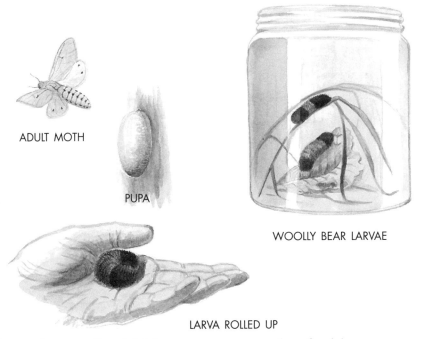

ADULT MOTH

PUPA

WOOLLY BEAR LARVAE

LARVA ROLLED UP

under a heap of rubbish, among a stack of old newspapers, under a rug, or even in a sneaker left in the garage.

Take a magnifying glass with you on your woolly-bear hunt. The little bears are interesting to see close up and are safe and easy to handle. Do not hesitate to pick one up. As soon as you do, it will roll into a ball. Then carefully replace it on the ground.

How long before the animal straightens out and begins to move? If it was moving when you found it, does it move in the same direction as before? Examine the front and hind legs. Can you find all eight pairs? When the woolly bear becomes an adult, it will have only three pairs of legs. Like all insects, the moth will have six legs.

You may wish to collect some woolly bears in a jar to observe indoors. Provide them with greens because they will continue to feed for some time. Toward springtime, the caterpillars will become quiet and spin cocoons. The adult moths will emerge in April.

Traveling Seeds

Through spring and summer and into fall, many plants produced flowers. After flowering, seeds developed, each containing a baby plant, ready to start a new generation of plants. Autumn is the time when the seeds containing these young plants leave their old neighborhoods to start life in a new place.

Each type of flower forms a different kind of fruit. Each fruit has one or more seeds. People eat many kinds of fruits, such as apples, oranges, and grapes. Birds, mice, and other animals may feed on these same fruits. They also feed on some fruits that people avoid, such as poisonous berries or the fruits of the dogwood tree.

Seeds get to their new homes in many different ways. Some travel only a short distance. An apple or an acorn, for instance, drops from its tree to the ground below. However, after the fruit rots, the exposed seed or seeds may be swept away by wind or rain, or an animal may eat the fruit. Although the animal digests the fruit, some of the seeds remain unchanged. These pass out of the animal's body with its waste and may take root where they fall.

Some seeds are carried in a very different way. They have spines or hooks that catch onto the fur and skin of animals. When the seeds fall or are rubbed off, they often take root where they have fallen.

Plan a safari to collect some of these traveling seeds. They are everywhere. Wear a pair of old, woolen socks on your hands. Sweep your hands through plants that have dried flowers. Many of the prickly fruits and seeds will stick to the socks. You may also discover some stuck to your clothes and even your hair.

Examine these hitchhikers. You may be familiar with the burdock fruits from a previous winter safari. They have seeds with sharp, little hooks that are very difficult to remove once they get onto clothing or fur. You may also find little green seedpods hanging on with their tiny hooks. These belong to a plant called tick trefoil. Other plant seeds may have two or four sharp hooks or other devices for hitching a ride. Their colorful common names describe them: Pitchforks, Spanish needles, cockleburs, and sticktights.

Wind is another means by which seeds are carried away from the parent plant. The tree fruits of maple, ash, linden, and pine have wings. So do the fruits of many other plants. The wings act as propellers to help the fruits fly to new places.

You have all seen dandelion fruits floating in the breeze. Each fruit contains one seed and is borne up by a little parachute. The fruits look like tiny, flying umbrellas.

Among the most attractive floating seeds are those of the milkweed. Find a closed, green pod. This is the milkweed fruit. Open it to see the beautiful arrangement of brown seeds with their attached silken parachutes. Late in the season, the darkened pods split open and the seeds float away–a beautiful sight against a blue sky.

There are additional means by which seeds are scattered in autumn. Plan safaris to nearby areas and discover the many ways that seeds are dispersed.

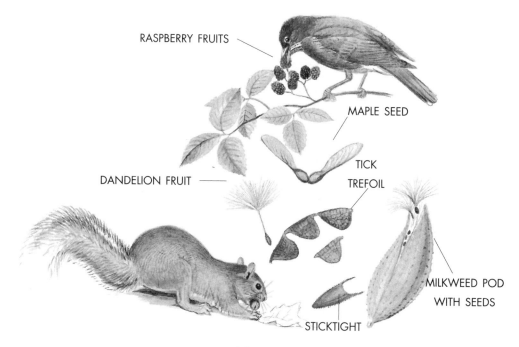

RASPBERRY FRUITS

MAPLE SEED

DANDELION FRUIT

TICK TREFOIL

MILKWEED POD WITH SEEDS

STICKTIGHT

An Autumn Egg Hunt

Many insects cannot survive the winter as adults. Before they die, they produce bunches of eggs that can withstand the cold weather. A good time to begin looking for these egg masses is in the late fall.

Plan to go on a fall safari to hunt for insect egg masses. One that is easily recognized is that of the gypsy moth. Batches of eggs may be found in many places, such as tree trunks, stones, and buildings. The straw-colored mass is rough to the touch. There may be five hundred eggs in one clump. Unfortunately, the gypsy moth larva feeds on the leaves of many of our trees and destroys them.

Look closely and you may see tiny, black creatures crawling among the eggs. These are wasps from Japan that have been imported to control the gypsy moth. They lay their eggs inside the moth eggs. The wasp eggs then hatch and destroy those of the gypsy moth.

Another common egg case is that of the tent caterpillar. These egg masses are found on a variety of trees and shrubs. Wild black cherry and apple are most frequently used. The dark, shiny, water-proof egg mass encircles a twig.

The praying mantis–a large, familiar insect–produces a fascinating case of eggs. The female may deposit as many as a thousand eggs on a twig, a board, or on the side of a building. She then covers the eggs with a frothy blanket, which hardens and protects them all winter.

A most interesting egg container is made by the bagworm. This insect makes a baglike case, about 1.5 inches (4 centimeters) long, in which it lives. It decorates the case with bits of leaves and twigs and suspends it in a tree by silken threads. Remove a bagworm case and cut it open to find the several hundred yellow eggs inside. If the bag is empty, it was occupied by a male. If you find eggs inside, the bag belonged to a female. The female bagworm cannot fly and never leaves her bag. Only the males fly.

You may find these and more kinds of egg cases when you go hunting for masses of eggs. This is an interesting and pleasant kind of safari for late autumn days.

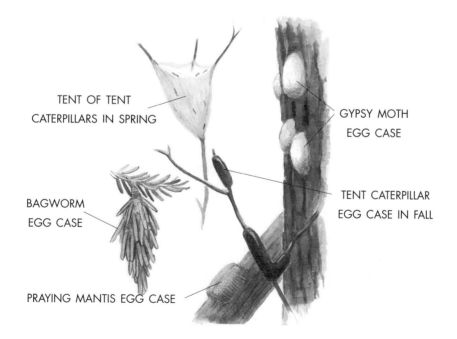

TENT OF TENT
CATERPILLARS IN SPRING

GYPSY MOTH
EGG CASE

TENT CATERPILLAR
EGG CASE IN FALL

BAGWORM
EGG CASE

PRAYING MANTIS EGG CASE

Spiders in the Air

A bright, autumn day is the best time to see ballooning spiders. Their silk streamers glisten in the sun and catch your eye. As these webs of silk float down, they are usually caught on trees, shrubs, and other tall plants. Some may even fall on your face. If you feel a tickle, you may find the spider that spun the silk. It will probably free itself and climb onto your finger. It will then spin threads for a new, silken balloon and try to sail again.

If you are fortunate enough to see these silken streamers, catch some on a twig. Point the twig up and you can watch the spider repeat its performance. Notice that the spider's head faces against the breeze. It raises the back part of its body and points it into the air. Then it spins a broad band of threads that forms a silken streamer. The band may be short or quite long.

The silken banner sways in the breeze and pulls the spider upward. When this happens the spider climbs up the silken threads and spins itself a basketlike seat. Secure in the basket, the spider goes ballooning wherever the breeze blows. If the spider wishes to stop, it gathers the threads under its jaws and forms them into a little, white ball. This makes the animal descend. It may fall on a plant, a person, or on the grass.

BALLOONING SPIDER

Sometimes the wind that carries the ballooning spiders is so strong it transports them many miles away. These little travelers have been found over the ocean and on ships far out at sea. Sometimes great numbers of ballooning spider threads are spun at the same time, and the wind blows them together to form sheets that spread over large areas. Look for such covers on the grass early in the morning. They will be covered with dew or frost and make a shining decoration in the sun.

A spider has special structures on the underside of the tip of its body. The structures, called spinnerets, spin out silk. The spinnerets are connected to glands inside the spider's body. There are different kinds of glands, and each makes a different type of silk. Some manufacture silk for making spiderwebs that are used to catch prey. Others produce a silk used for ballooning.

The silk leaves the spinnerets as a liquid. When the liquid comes in contact with the air, it hardens into strong threads. Think of the spinnerets as little spinning wheels.

Spiders do a lot of ballooning. They use this means of travel to get around. Most ballooning spiders are quite small. Thousands of young spiders go ballooning to locate new homes away from crowded areas. Some large spiders also use this method of transportation.

Plan several autumn safaris to watch ballooning spiders.

Tree Buds Wait for Spring

When autumn leaves fall, plants as well as animals prepare for winter. They must survive the cold weather in order to continue their lives the following spring. Trees wrap up their promises for next year's growth in their buds.

A tree's buds are already formed by the beginning of fall. Each variety of tree has its own kind of bud. A bud is a special structure with all its tiny growing parts folded up in a neat package.

The buds will open and grow into new parts of the tree when the next spring returns. Twigs, branches, flowers, and leaves all start as buds. The flowers will make new seeds. The new leaves will manufacture food for the growing tree. New twigs and branches will increase the tree's size.

Plan a safari to become acquainted with the different kinds of tree buds. They come in a variety of shapes, sizes, colors, and coverings. Your own backyard may have many varieties.

Red maple has little, round, red buds. Birches have pointed buds. The buds of sumac are woolly. Those of the horse chestnut are large, dark, and sticky. Remove one of these buds and open it very gently. You will see next year's leaves and flowers in miniature form.

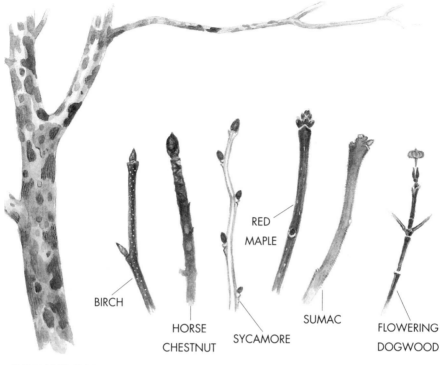

RED
MAPLE

BIRCH

HORSE
CHESTNUT

SYCAMORE

SUMAC

FLOWERING
DOGWOOD

SYCAMORE TREE

The flower buds of the flowering dogwood tree are easily recognized. They are shaped like miniature turnips and grow at the ends of twigs. The simple leaf buds grow along the twigs.

The sycamore tree is one of our tallest trees. You can recognize it by its colorful bark, which peels off in large pieces, revealing a trunk with a beautiful white, green, and yellow pattern. When you search for sycamore buds, you might think they are missing. This tree hides its buds. Remove a leaf with its stem, and you will find the bud. Notice that the end of the leaf stem, which is hollow, covers the bud.

You will probably find many other kinds of tree buds. They are all promises of spring.

Squirrel Watching

If you have but one tree in your backyard, you will surely find a gray squirrel living there, especially if it is a nut tree or an oak. You can discover much that is interesting about this lively, little animal. All you have to do is go outdoors and watch it. Gray squirrels are most active at sunrise and late in the afternoon. Plan your squirrel safaris for such times.

If you look carefully at the animal's fur, you will find other colors besides gray. Although it is mostly gray on top, it has some yellowish brown on its head and the sides of its body. Its undersides and the backs of its ears are mostly white. Notice the long, crinkly hairs on the squirrel's tail. They have bands of black, tan, and white.

Did you ever realize how noisy these animals are? They make many different sounds, and each sound has a special meaning. As you watch and listen, you can understand them. When they are excited they utter, "Cherk-cherk-cherk." When you or a strange squirrel approaches, you may hear teeth chattering. When a squirrel gets to know you or a friendly squirrel visits, listen for a purring sound. You will learn more about the squirrel's language. Just watch and listen.

The gray squirrel remains active all year. It does not hibernate, so it is very busy in the fall. It must prepare a nest and gather food for cold weather. It makes its winter nest in the upper branches of a tree. The nest looks like a large basketball made of leaves. You may even see the squirrel running up the trunk of the tree with a mouthful of leaves.

To prepare its winter food supply, it gathers acorns, nuts, and other ripe seeds, and stores them for later. Watch the squirrel's movements. If it is moving along slowly with its head close to the ground, it is searching for a meal. You may then observe how it holds what it has found and how it proceeds to eat it.

If a squirrel is storing food, it moves quickly. It holds the food in its mouth and searches for a bare spot in which to bury and hide it. It digs a little hole, drops the food into it, and then covers the food up. When the squirrel wants its buried meal, it seems to remember where to find it. Some people believe that squirrels can smell the food.

Plan to go squirrel watching around a bird feeder. You are sure to find more than one squirrel there. Besides observing some of their habits, you will discover new things on your own. Gray squirrels may seem tame when you are watching them, but you are really observing wild animals.

Singing Crickets

Crickets sing loudest in the fall. Autumn is mating time for crickets; it is also their singing time. Only the males sing. They sing to attract females. Of course, they do not sing in the same way that we do. Their song, more like a chirp, is made with their wings.

Crickets are abundant during this time of year. You can hear them everywhere. How do their musical instruments work? Plan a safari to find out. You can probably find several of the crickets in your own backyard or in a nearby field. Look under stones and in burrows. They feed on clover and grass. There are several kinds of crickets, but the black field cricket is the most common.

When a cricket is at rest, you see only the front pair of wings. A hind pair, which is used for flying, lies folded under the front wings. Males chirp with their front wings.

There is a narrow, rough place on each wing, which is called a file. When the cricket is ready to perform, it raises its front wings and rubs the file on one wing against the other wing. This produces the cricket's sound. It works somewhat like pulling a bow across a violin string. The female hears the music with her ears–which are found on her knees!

Insects were the world's first musicians. They began making music long before there were people or dinosaurs. Imagine being able to hear these same songs today.

Other insects besides crickets, such as grasshoppers and katydids, add to the autumn orchestra. Be sure to attend one or more of these musical events. The largest and loudest insect orchestras perform their symphonies at dusk.

FILE ON CRICKET'S WING

Witch Hazel Blossoms—
the Last Wildflowers of the Year

In the fall, when the trees are bare of leaves and the flowers have formed their seeds, the world of plants has a final surprise. To find this wonder, look for a tall shrub that grows in many yards, along roadsides, and in the woods. This plant is called the witch hazel, or witch of the woods. You will recognize it because it is the only shrub clothed in yellow blossoms so late in the season.

The witch hazel may burst into bloom after its leaves have turned yellow. Often, the leaves have already dropped. Little round buds open and flowers with four narrow yellow petals appear. The petals look like yellow streamers and give off a sweet perfume. If the weather should suddenly turn very cold, the petals curl up. A return of bright sunshine encourages them to open once more.

An interesting fruit pod develops on the witch hazel after it flowers. Examine the fruits closely to see their little monkey faces. When the pods dry, they split open. Each pod has two small, shiny black seeds. As the pod dries, it puts pressure on the seeds. The opening gets wider and the pressure increases. Finally the pressure is so great that it forces the seeds to shoot out. The seeds may fall some distance away from the plant. The process can be compared to shooting wet watermelon seeds by pressing them between your thumb and forefinger.

WITCH HAZEL FLOWERS

WITCH HAZEL
SEED POD, OPEN

DOWSING STICK

The scattering of the seeds among the dry autumn leaves produces a kind of muttering sound. People once thought that these sounds were made by witches, so they called the shrub the witch of the woods.

You can use the forked branches of witch hazel to make divining rods. A diviner, or a person who knows how to use such a rod, can locate an underground source of water. He or she might be hired by another person who wishes to have a well dug and wants to know the best place to dig it. The diviner holds the rod out in front with both hands and walks over the ground. The rod is supposed to dip down suddenly over a good water supply. Not all people believe this works, but many follow this method.

Witch hazel has been used for hundreds of years. The Indians and early settlers used the roots and twigs of the shrub for many home remedies.

The witch hazel plant is interesting for many reasons, especially because its golden blossoms appear late in the year when you would no longer expect to see wildflowers. Living things survive in many different and wonderful ways. One way or another, we are assured that life goes on. There is no beginning or end in nature.

Finding and observing the flowering and fruiting of the witch hazel plant is worth several safaris in the fall.

Additional Reading Suggestions

There are many interesting books that have more ideas for exploring and observing your world outdoors. Here are some to get you started:

Arnold, Caroline. *House Sparrows Everywhere.* San Diego: Carolrhoda, 1991.

Epple, Wolfgang. *Barn Owls.* San Diego: Carolrhoda, 1991.

Lawlor, Elizabeth. *Discover Nature Close to Home.* Harrisburg, Pa.: Stackpole, 1993.

Leslie, Clare W. *Nature All Year Long.* New York: Greenwillow, 1991.

Roth, Charles E. *The Wildlife Observer's Guidebook.* New York: Prentice Hall, 1982.

Shaffer, Carolyn, and Erica Fielder. *City Safaris.* San Francisco: Sierra Club Books, 1987.

Webster, David. *Exploring Nature Around the Year: Fall.* New York: Julian Messner, 1989.

——. *Exploring Nature Around the Year: Spring.* New York: Julian Messner, 1989.

——. *Exploring Nature Around the Year: Summer.* New York: Julian Messner, 1989.

——. *Exploring Nature Around the Year: Winter.* New York: Julian Messner, 1989.

There are many guidebooks to help you identify the variety of natural things you can find when you explore the outdoors. The *Golden Guides* are small books, which will fit easily in your pocket when you go on safaris. Here is a list of some of these titles:

Levi, Herbert W., and Lorna R. Levi. *Spiders and Their Kin.* Racine, Wis.: Golden Press, 1969.

Zim, Herbert S., and Clarence Cottam. *Insects.* Racine, Wis.: Golden Press, 1987.

Zim, Herbert S., and Ira N. Gabrielson. *Birds.* Racine, Wis.: Golden Press, 1956.

Zim, Herbert S., and Alexander C. Martin. *Trees.* Racine, Wis.: Golden Press, 1952.

Zim, Herbert S., and Robert Mitchell. *Butterflies and Moths.* Racine, Wis.: Golden Press, 1964.

Index

florets, 55–56
flowers, 41, 55, 69
  buds of, 82, 84, 111–12
  edible, 57
  evening-blooming, 82–84
  insects and, 40, 49, 83, 84, 109
  pixies in, 49–50
  seeds and, 56–57, 111–12, 119, 121,
    126
  see also wildflowers
flying squirrel, 61
food
  for birds, 24, 27, 32–33, 39, 48, 97
  for chipmunks, 101
  stored by chipmunks, 100
  stored by squirrels, 129
fossil fuel, 43
foxes, tracks of, 13
froghopper, 71–72
frogs, 37, 59, 61
  sounds of, 53–54, 69
fruits, 70, 105
  drinks made from, 115–16
  seeds of, 119–21
  yellow jackets and, 109
fungi, 29–30

glowworms, 75–77
golden beetles, 85–86
goldenrod, animals living in, 22–24
goldfinches
  feeding habits of, 33
  tracks of, 12
grapes, 119
grasshoppers, 131
gray squirrels, 128–29
groundhogs, 113–14
gypsy moths, eggs of, 122

hawks, 69
heat energy, 19
hedge bindweed, 85–86
hibernation
  of animals, 5, 113, 114

  of insects, 51, 117–18
  of turtles, 64
horse chestnut trees, 126
horses, tracks of, 13
horsetails, 41–43
house sparrows, 95–97

igloos, 20–21
Indians, 73–74, 115–16, 134
insects, 37, 51–52, 65, 70, 71-72,
  117–18
  colonies of, 44–45
  in dead trees, 60–61
  eggs of, 23–24, 51, 52, 76, 92, 93,
    108, 122–23
  elm trees and, 29–31
  flowers and, 40, 49, 83–84, 85-86,
    109
  glowing, 75–77
  hibernation of, 51, 117–18
  migration of, 5, 93–94
  molting of, 92, 99
  nectar-eating, 83, 84, 91
  in plants, 22–24
  on snow, 10–11
  sounds of, 58, 69, 98, 130–31
  stinging, 108–10
Isabella Tiger moth, 117, 118

Johnny-jump-ups, 50
juncos
  feeding habits of, 33
  tracks of, 12

katydids, 69, 98–99, 131

lady's nightcap, 85–86
larva, 117
  of ants, 44
  of butterflies, 51, 52
  of fireflies, 76
  of moths, 26, 117-18
  of peacock flies, 23–24
leaves, 105, 126